MW01242593

"I predict that *Where Will the M*[...] become an indispensable volum[...] the kind of insights - biblical a[...] [...] normally require a panel of authors. Dr. Travis' rich and varied experience as a pastor, bishop, and practicing attorney at law qualifies him to not only address such subjects as biblical models of succession, but also such topics as keys for proper transition from a legal and financial perspective. Bishop Travis successfully manages to bridge the spiritual to the practical. He deftly and articulately blends information with inspiration, provoking us to think, pray and plan. This book will be a classic because its content transcends the promise of its title. Yes, it is a book on succession planning, but the astute pastor will also find in it a wonderful primer for mentoring the next generation of leaders on what it takes to be a successful successor. Bishop Travis has dug a well of knowledge by which future generations will be enriched. Thank you, sir!"

BISHOP MARK A. MOORE, SR.
FOUNDING PASTOR, FAITH COVENANT CHURCH, ATLANTA, GA
HOST, YOU CAN GET THERE FROM HERE VISIONARIES CONFERENCE

"Bishop T. Travell Travis, Esq. has done it again. *Where Will the Mantle Fall* is unequivocally a masterpiece and true work of art on the undeveloped and unprescribed subject of succession planning. It's truly amazing that such an important subject has gone under the radar for so long. However, this book wrestles the conversation to the forefront of a just and thorough examination. Essentially, through this literary work we learn success is truly not success without succession. Every church in this nation who truly cares about its congregants owes it to themselves to get this book and apply its principles to ensure that the gospel of Jesus Christ and his mission to serve mankind through the vehicle of his church will not only continue through succession but get stronger from generation to generation. Don't delay in getting this book as it holds the keys to your ministry's future."

PASTOR JAY PATRICK
FOUNDING PASTOR, LIBERATION CHURCH, RICHMOND, VA
HOST, CHURCH BUILDERS SUMMIT AND CHURCH BUILDERS NETWORK

"Bishop T. Travell Travis, Esq. is one of America's rising voices for such a time as this. He is a real knowledgeable and humble servant of God. This book is a must read for all pastors, denominations, parachurch leaders, business owners and executives. His insight as a pastor and attorney was captured in this book, teaching us the biblical and legal side of succession planning. This book also helps us avoid the pitfalls of succession planning and prepares us to achieve lasting legacies."

BISHOP MICHAEL PENN
PASTOR, THE GALILEAN HOUSE OF WORSHIP, MARTINSVILLE, VA
FOUNDER, THE LEAGUE OF INDEPENDENT MINISTERS

WHERE WILL THE
MANTLE
FALL?

A Biblical and Legal Guide to Succession Planning

TORRINO TRAVELL TRAVIS

DEDICATION

This book is dedicated to all the men and women of God that have impacted my life and have gone on to be with the Lord. I pray that every day they find a return on their investment in me. This book is also dedicated to those who passed away during the pandemic of 2020 and to Covid-19. I pray that the memories and mantles left behind have fallen into good hands.

IN LOVING MEMORY
Bishop Keith Darrell Nesmith
September 2, 1958 - November 26, 2019

Mother Cecilia Coleman Williams
November 2, 1939 - April 20, 2020

ACKNOWLEDGMENTS

I give God all the glory, honor, and praise for everything. If I could sing, I would sum up my testimony with two songs: "Jesus is the Best Thing That Ever happened to Me!" and "Jesus Made Something Beautiful Out of My Life!" My ultimate desire in life is not just to hear God say, "Well done," but to also hear Him say, "This is my beloved son, in whom I am well pleased!"

The scripture informs us that "every good and every perfect gift is from above" (James 1:17 KJV). For that reason, I am indeed grateful for my good and perfect gift, my wife, Sherina. Before she knew that the Lord was dealing with me about writing a second book, one day in service earlier this year, the Lord laid it on her heart to kneel in front of me and to pray for me. While I don't remember everything she said that day, I do recall one specific prayer; she told me to write, because God has given me more to share with His people. Without her prayers, patience, and support, this book would never have been written. To my three champions: Deonna (2009), Janiyah (2010), and Amiyah (2018); thank you for being my biggest cheerleaders. Every day you motivate me to be a better husband, father and servant of God. I pray that I will leave you a legacy that will always make you proud. To my mother Cassandra Johnson Travis, and grandmother, Nadine Dillard Johnson: I pray that I always make you proud and that you will continue to reap the benefits from the sacrifices you made to help me become who I am today.

I am grateful for the outstanding support staff God provided to help write and publish this book. First, I want to thank my writing consultant and editor Dr. Dana Tyler. Your words of wisdom, encouragement and professional advice, both before and during this process, helped make this book a reality. In addition, I want to thank the esteemed group of pastors who took time out of their busy schedules to review the unpublished manuscript and provide constructive feedback. I am eternally indebted to Bishop Mark A.

Moore, Sr., Bishop Michael Penn, and Pastor Jay Patrick. Thank you for your friendship, mentorship, encouragement and feedback. By providing space on your platform to share with other pastors, I was inspired and equipped to write this book. May God continue to bless your lives, ministries and families! Last but not least, I want to thank my graphic designer, Pastor NaTasha Heath-Ashton and Ashton Creative Group. Your creativity, patience, and professionalism kept me motivated towards completing this book. I pray that this book becomes a blessing to your business.

I want to acknowledge my father in the gospel, Bishop Earley Dillard and home church, Shiloh Way of the Cross Church, in Martinsville, VA. To my Presiding Bishop, Bishop Alphonzo D. Brooks, Presiding Bishop Emeritus, Apostle Leroy H. Cannady, Sr., and the members of The Way of the Cross Church of Christ International. I am eternally grateful for the international church family that God gave to this only-child from a small town, low-income, single-parent household. Lastly, to the church that God has blessed me to establish and pastor since 2009, City of Refuge Way of the Cross Church, Richmond, VA. – the best is yet to come!

Finally, I want to thank all of the pastors and leaders that either directly or indirectly have taught, mentored, inspired and motivated me. Moreover, I especially want to thank those who have given me the opportunity to provide legal services. I would not have been able to write this book without the experience you afforded me or the revelation and understanding of scriptures imparted to me. May your ministries and mantles fall into the right hands!

IN REMEMBRANCE OF

I have dedicated this book to honor the life and legacy of two very influential people in my life who recently passed away: Bishop Keith D. Nesmith and Mother Cecilia C. Williams.

BISHOP KEITH D. NESMITH served as pastor of Greater St. Peter Way of the Cross Church, Andrews, South Carolina. He also served as the 7th president of the International Youth for Christ. I met Bishop Nesmith, at age 13 when I was just elected to my first position with the International Youth for Christ- as vice president of the intermediate (teen) youth. At the time, Bishop Nesmith was the 2nd Vice President and responsible for the intermediate youth. At my first national meeting in office, Bishop Nesmith handed me the mic and gave me the opportunity to preside over the intermediate service. Bishop Nesmith would later become president and I would serve as his second vice president.

When I became president, he became my primary advisor. Without Bishop Nesmith, I would not have become a pastor, IYFC president, or even married my wife, Sherina. Countless times, Bishop Nesmith would open up his home, pulpit, and even loan me his nice new Cadillac, so that I could travel throughout the state of South Carolina to minister to our churches. We've spent countless hours discussing my many questions about life, ministry, and family. Even when his health declined, if he knew I was anywhere in South Carolina, he would either meet my wife and me for dinner or surprise us by attending the service. I would not be who I am today without God placing Bishop Keith D. Nesmith in my life as a teenager.

MOTHER CECILIA C. WILLIAMS served as the founding mother of Mission of Love Way of the Cross Church in Philadelphia, PA. For nearly 30 years, she would serve as national missionary president for The Way of the Cross Church of Christ, International. Most notably, she was the mother of 9 children, 31 grandchildren and 21 great-grandchildren with my wife being the oldest grandchild. My wife not only grew up in her grandparents' church, but she lived with her grandparents while she attended West Chester University. Before I met my wife, Bishop and Mother Williams adopted me as a member of their family. Shortly after preaching my initial sermon, one of the first people to invite me to come and speak at their church was Mother Williams, to celebrate her birthday. Today, my wife walks in her legacy as a mother, First Lady and officer in our national church. Even in her declining health, Mother Williams always found the strength to attend my wife's graduations or special events at our church. At her last convocation in 2019, Mother Williams was able to witness her granddaughter serve as a featured Women's Day speaker and become the first woman elected to the office of 2nd Vice President of the International Youth for Christ. Not only did she train my wife well, but her advice, encouragement and prayers have helped us both to become who we are today. Indeed, Mother William's mantle is in good hands with her granddaughter.

TABLE OF CONTENTS

INTRODUCTION

On the day that I began writing this book, my wife and I were living in separate rooms, away from our children, because we both had tested positive for Covid-19. My wife's grandmother would spend a week in the hospital with Covid-19, beat it and be released from the hospital, but due to other medical issues, pass away. Not only were we under quarantine, but my mother-in-law was in the hospital, my father-in-law was quarantined, and my three daughters were fending for themselves in the house even while they rotated having fevers. My wife's aunt, along with my two sisters-in-law would have Covid-19 as well as others in my wife's family. It is during this six-week period of shut-down, quarantine, and isolation in the spring 2020, that I was able to complete the first draft of this book. Nothing makes you stop procrastinating or thinking about your own mortality more than being diagnosed with a once-a-century deadly virus. But thanks be to God! He kept us, healed us, and gave me the ability to finish this book!

Over the last fifteen years, I have been blessed to practice law helping pastors, entrepreneurs, creatives, and members of the community. One of the most memorable clients came very early in my career; he was a pastor. As a child, my home church would have service with his church on a regular basis. Whether it was a district service, diocese meeting, youth conference, convocation, fellowship service, anniversary, revival, fish-fry, you name it, our churches were together! However, because I was a youth, I never had an extended conversation with the pastor. After being away for four years of college, three years of law school, and some years living out of town, I received an urgent call that he needed to meet with me.

I knew the pastor had become ill but learned that he was in the final stages of cancer. He was a successful pastor, entrepreneur, and had several children. However, he did not have an estate or succession plan in place. Although his body was weak, his mind was still very sharp. For about two hours, I sat by his bedside discussing his desires, concerns, and options regarding his church, business, and family. I recall the mixed emotions that day: honored to serve him at this most critical moment; concerned that it was too much to discuss with him in this condition and saddened by the inevitability of his demise.

The following week, I met with him in the hospital with his key staff to review and sign the documents I had crafted for him. Two weeks later, we held his funeral. Cutting it close is an understatement. On one hand, he was fortunate that because of his condition, he knew that he did not have much time left and was able to put something in writing for his church and family. However, not every pastor has this "luxury" and may end up passing away without anything in place for their families or congregation. Over the next decade, our church body would have nearly one-fourth of our pastors pass away. I never envisioned that my job as Way of the Cross Church - International Youth for Christ president would entail giving remarks at so many funeral services. Some churches had smooth, if not seamless transitions while others, unfortunately, had tumultuous, if not catastrophic, transitions between leaders.

Pastors and leaders, just imagine for a moment the first Sunday after your funeral. Who will be the speaker? Who will make the decision that they would be the speaker on that Sunday? Who will show up to church that Sunday and continue to support the ministry in the future? Will your spouse and children be taken care of emotionally, spiritually, and financially? Does the church have a process, protégé, or pool of qualified candidates that could become the next pastor? Who will be in charge of the selection process? Will there be a vote? Who gets to vote? Will the next pastor be successful?

A pastor may not be able to control everything that happens after they pass away. However, a pastor should prepare his church and family for the inevitability of their death. Whether the successor builds up, tears

2

down, or simply maintains the church is largely contingent upon a well-crafted, designed, and implemented succession plan.

Moreover, when we think of succession planning in the church, we tend to only think of it in the event of the pastor's death. However, succession planning should occur at all levels for all positions in the church. Whether at a denominational level, local church level, or auxiliary level, within a church, every position should have someone trained to step in to fill a position in a moment's notice.

Succession planning is not just about planning for someone to die. For various reasons people become unable to serve in a position in a church. Succession planning is needed in death, but it could be utilized in sickness, age, term-limits, or boredom. A member could have a change in work responsibilities, marital status, or family obligations. It is not uncommon for someone to relocate to another city due to a denominational assignment, career opportunity, family obligation, or personal preference. Change is inevitable! Unless the rapture takes place, death is inevitable! Furthermore, the days of someone spending their entire life with one church are over.

Surely as the world turns and seasons change, your church will also experience changes in membership and leadership over time. Reality check: people resign from positions, people leave churches; people leave town; people leave God; and people pass away. However, the church has to be in a position to keep the bus moving and on schedule, even if passengers board and exit the bus on a regular basis.

Therefore, like a good football team, the church has to train and develop people for every position and have them ready to serve, even if it is only in a moment's notice. Whether this person succeeds, maintains, or fails is often predicated on the amount of training and preparation that took place before their "moment" arrived.

In this book, we will discuss examples of both successful and unsuccessful transitions in leadership. We will also discuss the characteristics of a good successor, the importance of mentorship and training for a protege, and the role nepotism often plays in succession planning. The book will conclude with a discussion of the legal aspect of an estate plan, preparing for disability, retirement, and ultimately death. At the end of the book, we provide a succession planning checklist, sample succession bylaws and a successor evaluation. Prayerfully, by the end of the book you will be equipped to prepare yourself, your family, your congregation, and your successor for the inevitable transition in pastoral leadership.

CHAPTER 1

WHAT ARE SUCCESSION PLANS AND THE REASONS LEADERS FAIL TO PLAN FOR SUCCESSION?

"I PLAY A COMPLICATED POSITION IN AN INTENSELY TEAM-ORIENTED GAME."
~ TOM BRADY

Following a seven-season postseason drought, the New England Patriots selected Drew Bledsoe as the first overall pick in the 1993 NFL Draft. Overnight, Bledsoe would become the face of the franchise and lead the Patriots to four playoff appearances and the Super Bowl in 1996. However, in 2001, after a decline in performance, two consecutive seasons without a playoff appearance, and a near fatal injury, Drew Bledsoe was replaced as starter by an untested, 6-round, second-year backup quarterback, by the name of Tom Brady. Brady was thrust into the season opener to play the final 2:16 of a 10-3 loss to the New York Jets. Bledsoe would never play another game for the Patriots. Overlooked by many scouts because of his less than stellar physical abilities; Tom Brady soon developed a reputation for his "work ethic, pocket awareness, and intelligence."

After taking over for Bledsoe, in his first season at quarterback, Brady would lead the Patriots on an improbable run to the Super Bowl with an upset victory over the heavily favored Saint Louis Rams. Over the next 20 years, Brady would lead the Patriots to 9 Super Bowl appearances, 6 Super Bowl victories, 17 division titles, a 16-game perfect regular season, and a winning season each year while starting at quarterback. Today, many would consider Tom Brady the greatest quarterback of all time!

As a pastor, can any of your ministers come "off the bench" in an instant and lead your church to a Super Bowl victory in their first year or better yet, become a historic dynasty over the next 20 years? Having a succession plan is all about having a backup quarterback ready to successfully lead the team in a moment's notice. If one can appreciate that concept when it comes to football, how much more should it be embraced when it comes to the church?

Management guru Peter Drucker once said, "There is no success without a successor." Leadership expert and author of the famed book, *The 21 Irrefutable Law of Leadership's Law of Legacy,* John Maxwell wrote, "A leader's lasting value is measured by succession." As pastors, one is in the business of preparing individuals for life after death. However, many pastors are unwilling to prepare for their own death. Preparing for death is not only a spiritual matter, but also a legal and financial matter for the pastor's family and church.

While the Bible says that we may reach three score and ten or by reason of strength reach four score the reality is that pastors are dying much younger and for a myriad of reasons. No longer is pastoring known as the profession that affords the longest life for its members. Some pastors may live to get very old, but many also will die young, unexpectedly, or all of a sudden.

Thus, the questions must be asked: what will happen to me, my family, or my ministry if I become incapacitated, disabled, retired, pass away or simply decide to quit or resign? Who will be in charge? Who will decide who will take charge? Are they prepared to lead? Will my family be taken care of financially for the foreseeable future?

Essentially, the future of your ministry in the hands of your successor will have one of three outcomes: maintain the ministry, build-up the ministry, or tear-down the ministry. This is your life's work or legacy; thus, a leader should not want to see it destroyed when they die. In fact, a good leader should want to see the ministry grow, flourish, and prosper after his death. As a leader, have you done everything within your power to

6

ensure the success of the ministry after your season or tenure has ended? Even if the next leader is an epic failure, let it not be because the previous leader did not position him and the church for success to excel in the future.

Depending on your church polity or governing structure: congregational, Presbyterian, episcopal, authoritarian, autocratic, or theocratic, etc., it may not ultimately be your decision to select your successor. Some churches operate more like a democracy while others operate more like a monarchy. This is not to judge any form of church government as superior to the other, but the form of government a church has will impact how succession planning is designed and implemented in a particular church. For example, under congregational governance, as many traditional Baptist churches may follow, the church is already established and the church board decides when to hire, retire, fire or replace the pastor. Whereas under an episcopal governance, the leadership of the respective denomination that the church is affiliated, will assign, replace, and even compensate the new pastor.

However, under these church polities a leader can often, depending on their tenure, exercise a hand in developing a pool of potential successors, ensure that bylaws are up-to-date, and that the church bylaws clearly address the questions of succession. In a church where it is not up to the pastor, alone, to decide on a successor - as a pastor or leader, have you prepared and positioned the protégé in such a way that they will be the clear choice to the congregation? Further, a pastor should be an example of godly leadership, handling both the temporal and spiritual affairs of the church well, and by preparing the congregation to receive the next leader, whoever that person might be. Pastors can leave a church in "good shape" or in a "total mess"; either way, it will have a major impact on the success of the next pastor.

Under a more apostolic form of church government, the voice of the pastor, especially if the pastor is the founder of the church, will have significant, if not absolute authority, when naming the successor for the church. Even under this form of church government, a leader should have

7

carefully crafted, legally sound process, or affidavit, and put in writing identifying who they have selected as the next pastor. It is imperative for the leader to prepare the protégé to lead and the people to receive and follow the next leader. Otherwise, what the leader says may in fact "go" for that church, but it may also mean that the people "go" or in other words leave, if they are not satisfied with who was selected as successor.

Succession planning is more than just a pastoral-level matter. Succession planning must be thought about at every level and for every position in the church. Whether it is a church officer, ministry or auxiliary leader, choir director, musician, sound technician, or nursery worker. Any given Sunday, for any given reason, a church should be able to say "next man up" and keep the ministry afloat or hold down a position until the person returns, or until someone is trained more to fulfil the position, or God sends a permanent replacement. For any reason, and at any time, someone should be prepared to come off the bench, fill in as quarterback, and lead the team to victory – perhaps, even a couple Super Bowl championships!

The following is a list of ten common reasons pastors do not engage in succession planning. The list is not exhaustive or in any particular rank or order but provides insight into why leaders often do not engage in succession planning.

1. PROCRASTINATION AND IMMORTALITY:

A wise preacher once stated while making an altar call, "Today is the tomorrow; that you talked about yesterday." How many of us put off until tomorrow the things God is telling us to do today? Most pastors place great value on timeliness, seasons, and operating without hesitation to the urgent prompting of the Holy Spirit – except when it comes to taking care of their own bodies or planning their temporal affairs.

"I'll go to the doctor next week!"

"I'll take a vacation next year!"

"I'll put together an estate plan before my next birthday!"

"I'll put together a succession plan after my next pastoral anniversary!"

James 4:13-14 (NIV) reminds us "Now listen, you who say, 'Today or tomorrow we will go to this or that city, spend a year there, carry on business and make money.' Why, you do not even know what will happen tomorrow. What is your life? You are a mist that appears for a little while and then vanishes."

Not to be morbid, but every day we are reminded of pastors, athletes, and entertainers who in their prime were taken away from us prematurely. The notion of preparing for life after death is a sobering thought for anyone. Accidents, unexpected tragedies, unknown illness, and even unprecedented pandemics can prevent a pastor from reaching the blessed age of three score and ten. Even so, what if the pastor becomes disabled or is led to resign or to retire? You may know pastors who had everything in place both spiritually and naturally and know of pastors who died without a plan for anything. As a result, their spouse, family, and church may suffer because the pastor didn't have any of his stuff in order!

As you read this book, you may be left with the opportunity to determine if you will be known as one that had it all together or the one that had nothing together As many pastors would conclude their altar call, I say to you: if you hear the voice of God, harden not your heart. Today, the choice is yours!

2. INDECISIVENESS

Perhaps you may be a pastor unsure, undecided, or simply God has not revealed a person or a process for succession. If a successor is named publicly or prematurely, one might also be concerned with the reaction of the individual, the congregation, or those not selected. Also, a pastor might be afraid that if they name someone today, but 30 years later they believe someone else should fill the position, that they cannot change it.

A young pastor should have a person or process in place now, but if necessary, also have the ability to change it thirty years from now. No one knows who God might save, send, or call to the ministry during a pastor's tenure. Thus, under this scenario, it might be better to give someone a title such as assistant pastor with the bylaws, providing for the person to become interim or acting pastor, but still require the candidate to go through a selection process before they officially become the next pastor. This would allow the individual to become the presumptive nominee, but not the automatic nominee, with other candidates being included in the selection process.

An alternate framework may call for the pastor to appoint and if not, then the selection process provision would "kick-in" and make the determination. A similar analogy would be the succession plan for the president of the United States. Upon the resignation, disability, or death of a president, the vice president automatically becomes president. However, if they want their own term as president, they have to undergo the nomination process and be elected by the people to serve a full term.

Regardless of the manner in which it is done, indecisiveness or fear of being "locked-in" to a particular person should not be an excuse from crafting a succession plan. If drafted correctly, a succession plan can give the leader a plan for "now," but also the flexibility to create a new plan for "later."

3. AMBIVALENCE AND NEGLIGENCE

"So, they were scattered, because there was no shepherd, and they became food for all the wild beasts. My sheep were scattered; they wandered over all the mountains and on every high hill. My sheep were scattered all over the face of the earth, with none to search or seek for them." Ezekiel 34:5-6 (ESV)

Three times, Jesus asked Peter, if Peter loved him. "When they had finished eating, Jesus said to Simon Peter, "Simon son of John, do you love me more than these?" "Yes, Lord," he said, "you know that I love you." Jesus said, "Feed my lambs." Again, Jesus said, "Simon son of John, do you love me?" He answered, "Yes, Lord, you know that I love you." Jesus said, "Take care of my sheep." The third time he said to him, "Simon son of John, do you love me?" Peter was hurt because Jesus asked him the third time, "Do you love me?" He said, "Lord, you know all things; you know that I love you." Jesus said, "Feed my sheep." (John 21:15-17 NIV)

The legal definition of negligence is "A failure to behave with the level of care that someone of ordinary prudence would have exercised under the same circumstances. The behavior usually consists of actions, but can also consist of omissions when there is some duty to act"[1]

It is hard to imagine that if God called one to pastor a flock that he would allow that individual to leave the flock without a shepherd. One cannot make any sheep stay with any particular flock, but unless you are a mere hireling; to intentionally leave a congregation without a pastor is tantamount to negligence, malfeasance, and dereliction of duty. Unfortunately, some pastors have misinterpreted and even misapplied what Jesus said in Mark 10:40 (KJV), "but to sit on my right hand and on my left is not mine to give, but it is for those for whom it is prepared" as a reason not to engage in succession planning. For the sake of modesty and even humor: as important as one might see themselves and their position as pastor, we are not dealing with the throne of Christ!

Even if it is ultimately not your "duty" to select one's successor, a pastor can still begin the process of grooming a protégé to lead and preparing the congregation to receive their next shepherd. A pastor can help craft a selection process; train a pool of protégés; leave the church in good financial standing; develop a healthy church culture; and be an example of what it means to be a good pastor. In this way, hopefully, you will ensure a smooth transition and position the next pastor to succeed.

4. IGNORANCE

This word is not to be taken as offensive or insulting. It simply means that one is not aware of the need or does not know how to do a particular thing. For some pastors, terms such as succession planning,

---

[1] https://www.law.cornell.edu/wex/negligence

11

bylaws, article of incorporation, powers of attorney, and 401(k) plan is not a part of their regular vocabulary. Alternatively, we tend to do things as we see them done. Thus, in the old church there was less need for bylaws because whatever "Bishop said" was the law! Many things that the old church may have gotten away with in the past would definitely lead to a lawsuit in today's church. Even those who may have attended seminary or even business school have not been taught about succession planning. If you lack knowledge or awareness of a succession plan, then this book is written for you! Prayerfully by the time you finish reading this book, you will be informed and empowered to create a succession plan that is both biblically and legally sound.

5. FEAR

"Nothing that I had worked for and earned meant a thing to me, because I knew that I would have to leave it to my successor, and he might be wise, or he might be foolish—who knows? Yet he will own everything I have worked for, everything my wisdom has earned for me in this world. It is all useless. So, I came to regret that I had worked so hard." (Ecclesiastes 2:18-20 GNT - emphasis added).

It is not uncommon for a leader to feel the same way as King Solomon. Fear of turning one's life work over to another individual while not knowing what they will do with it. Fear of not knowing how the protégé will respond to knowing that they are the "chosen one" to be the successor. Fear of not knowing how the congregation will react to your much carefully thought after and prayed over decision. Will those who are not selected revolt and turn against you?[2] Fear of even being forgotten as a leader and one's accomplishments being erased from history.

---

[2] "When the enemies of Judah and Benjamin heard that the exiles were building a temple for the LORD, the God of Israel, they came to Zerubbabel and to the heads of the families and said, "Let us help you build because, like you, we seek your God and have been sacrificing to him since the time of Esarhaddon king of Assyria, who brought us here." But Zerubbabel, Joshua and the rest of the heads of the families of Israel answered, "You have no part with us in building a temple to our

In the end, one cannot determine whether people will remember or forget them when they retire or pass away. However, a pastor who has done the work of the Lord can take consolation in knowing that God will never forget them or their efforts to serve God's people. Hebrews 6:10 (NIV) "God is not unjust; he will not forget your work and the love you have shown him as you have helped his people and continue to help them." In the end, it matters less who does not remember you, as long as God never forgets you!

6. PRIDE AND EGO

"Pride is an unreasonable feeling of superiority and is an inwardly directed emotion with a negative connotation. It is a higher opinion of one's self. Pride refers to a foolish, irrational, and corrupt sense of one's personal value, status, or accomplishments. The spirit of pride seeks to be equal with God. It is imperative to ask God in times of prayer and personal reflection to expose all forms of pride, haughtiness and arrogance that is hidden in our hearts...

It is a fervent quest to be acknowledged and see because of an exaggerated sense of self...an excessive need to be ostentatious and boastful especially concerning one's possessions, looks and achievements. This also means having or showing arrogant superiority and an obvious disdain for people viewed less worthy or beneath them....often they are masterful at making people feel inadequate and insufficient. Additionally, like the proud and haughty heart, arrogance is having a super exaggerated

---

God. We alone will build it for the LORD, the God of Israel, as King Cyrus, the king of Persia, commanded us." **Then the peoples around them set out to discourage the people of Judah and make them afraid to go on building. They bribed officials to work against them and frustrate their plans during the entire reign of Cyrus king of Persia and down to the reign of Darius king of Persia."** (Ezra 4:1-5 NIV - emphasis added)

sense of one's own importance, gifts, or abilities. This kind of heart causes a self-important, snooty and vain spirit." [3]

Do you believe that no one can do what you've done or that no one can do it better than you? Are your thoughts eerily similar to King Nebuchadnezzar "...Is not this the great Babylon I have built as the royal residence, by my mighty power and for the glory of my majesty?" (Daniel 4:30 NIV - emphasis added)

True, no one can replace you as a leader or duplicate your achievements; but it is more dangerous to think or assume that no one else can get the job done other than you. Surely as the world turns, and seasons come and go, one way or the other, one day you will be replaced by someone. A successor will have their own unique combination of skills and abilities as well as their own set of strengths and weaknesses for the job. If a church cannot survive past the death of the pastor, then perhaps it was never structured to be a church but structured as a ministry of the pastor.

The question is whether the leader is proactive in preparing their successor to do the job or are they leaving it up to their successor to figure it out all on their own. Failure to prepare a successor is tantamount to setting up the successor to fail. If a successor fails, it is often just as much the failure of the leader as it is on the protégé. For many leaders it takes a career or lifetime to learn the tough lessons of leadership. As a pastor prepares for succession, he/she can assist the leader in avoiding most, if not all, these tough lessons of leadership. If done properly, a leader can catapult their successor into a bright and successful future.

7. INCOME SECURITY

While money matters, money should not be the sole factor in determining how long one stays in a position, especially as pastor. It's one thing to preach until you die, but do you have to pastor until you die? Unfortunately, for many pastors the option to retire is not feasible because

---

[3] Excerpts from "Day 8: The Proud and Haughty Heart" of *The Heart Monitor* by Kimberly Ray-Gavin © 2018 by Kim Ray-Gavin.

of financial reasons. Either they are dependent on the salary or feel entitled to the salary for the years of service where they did not get compensated or were undercompensated. With a decline in physical or mental capabilities, pastors may struggle to pastor a flock to their peril but also to the peril of their congregation. It takes early and careful retirement planning to ensure that a pastor can afford to retire if or whenever they might need to or desire. Likewise, or alternatively, it takes careful planning for a church to afford to pay two salaries, one for the former pastor, and one for the new pastor. Yet with a well-crafted compensation package a church and pastor can put in place provisions, so that the pastor has the option to retire. Retirement will be discussed more in Chapter 13: When to Hang Up the Cleats?

8. JEALOUSY AND INSECURITY

"Whatever mission Saul sent him on, David was so successful that Saul gave him a high rank in the army. This pleased all the troops, and Saul's officers as well.

When the men were returning home after David had killed the Philistine, the women came out from all the towns of Israel to meet King Saul with singing and dancing, with joyful songs and with timbrels and lyres. As they danced, they sang:

"Saul has slain his thousands, and David his tens of thousands." Saul was very angry; this refrain displeased him greatly. "They have credited David with tens of thousands," he thought, "but me with only thousands. What more can he get but the kingdom?" And from that time on Saul kept a close eye on David. Saul was afraid of David, because the LORD was with David but had departed from Saul. When Saul saw how successful he was, he was afraid of him. But all Israel and Judah loved David, because he led them in their campaigns...When Saul realized that the LORD was with David and that his daughter Michal loved David, Saul became still more afraid of him, and he remained his enemy the rest of his days. Saul told his son Jonathan and all the attendants to kill David. But Jonathan had taken a great liking to David" (I Samuel 18:5-9, 12, 14-15, 28-29, 19:1 NIV)

Should Saul have been so insecure when the women sang David's praises that it made him turn against his greatest asset, David due to jealousy? Not only did Saul lose the kingdom, his legacy, and ultimately his life; Saul also lost the love, loyalty, and respect of his children. Both Micah and Jonathan would aid David in escaping from their father, Saul. Solomon sums up jealousy this way, "...for love is strong as death; jealousy is cruel as the grave: the coals thereof are coals of fire, which hath a most vehement flame." (Songs of Solomon 8:6 KJV).

Why should Moses be jealous of Joshua for carrying the people into the Promise Land? Why should David be jealous of Solomon for building the palace, the temple and having peace during his reign? Why should Elijah be jealous of Elisha for performing twice as many miracles? Jesus said to his disciples, "greater works shall you do in my name". A leader should not worry about who gets the credit as long as the job gets done! If the next leader enjoys state-of-the art facilities, larger salary, increased membership, or greater notoriety – rejoice and be glad! A successor should not have to waste valuable time repairing or rebuilding a foundation that their predecessor neglected or tore apart; but a successor should be able to build on a solid foundation and take the ministry to the next dimension.

Antithetical to Saul, Paul writes to the church at Corinth, I Corinthians 3:3-9 (NIV),"I planted the seed, Apollos watered it, but God has been making it grow. So, neither the one who plants nor the one who waters is anything, but only God, who makes things grow. The one who plants and the one who waters have one purpose, and they will each be rewarded according to their own labor. For we are co-workers in God's service; you are God's field, God's building."

What if Saul had treated David as Paul treated Apollos? A good pastor should want to see the work of the Lord carried on in their absence and not fall apart after their death. A good pastor does not want to juxtapose their accomplishments against the failures of their successor in order to prove their value or cement their legacy. A good leader embraces and celebrates their David and does not try to sabotage or kill him. Ultimately, a good leader should set up their successor to succeed!

9. LOSS OF CONTROL

Many pastors do not want to confront the question – "Who am I when I am no longer the pastor?" Most leaders, no matter how tired, frustrated, and ready to quit they may be at the time; deep down, most love the feeling of being in charge. If they could set-aside the stress and drama of leadership, most leaders love casting vision, giving directions, having influence, retaining visibility, and commanding respect. All this can be summed up in one word – relevance! "Will I become irrelevant if I step down as pastor of the church?"

Pastors can become so enamored with seeing their name on the building, picture on the flyer, the big seat in the pulpit, and having the final say on matters; that the mere thought of losing that relevance scares them to death (no pun intended). Sadly, some pastors have pastored so long that they have lost their identity or cannot separate who they are from what they do. A preacher's title might change over time, but the name on one's birth certificate remains the same. Paul never referred to himself as Apostle Paul but as "Paul, an apostle of Jesus Christ." "Pastor," "Bishop," "Apostle" may be your office, position or title, but it is not your name or the sole basis of your identity. A leader can get so used to hearing and responding to "Bishop" that they forget their own name. Just because Sarah called Abraham "lord" does not mean that your spouse or your children must always refer to you by your ecclesiastical title. I quite honestly doubt that one's name written in the "Lamb's Book of Life" has a title included[4]. It is

---

[4] It is improper to sign one's name with a title included. The title can be included on the signature line but should not be included with the actual signature. One's name and signature does not change. It remains the same regardless of title or position. For example: *Torrino Travell Travis* / **Bishop T. Travell Travis, Esq., Pastor**

fundamental that pastors never forget the distinction between "who I am" and "what I am!"

If losing control is an issue, a well-crafted succession plan, can be fundamental to orchestrating a smooth or gradual transition of leadership. The plan could provide the retiring pastor to have a limited but crucial role in the leadership of the church. By the same token, God can give solace to a leader in being content with the completion of their assignment or by pursuing a new role or a different assignment in the Kingdom. Whenever the master decides to remove us: whether by reassignment, retirement, or death; it is ultimately God's decision, not ours. In the end, being a pastor is a privilege and not a right. God owns the church and merely gives pastors the opportunity to care for it until He returns for it.

10. OPPORTUNE MOMENT

Perhaps none of the aforementioned reasons apply to you. However, you are simply waiting on the correct timing to announce a succession plan or successor. For Moses, God did not reveal who his successor would be until his death. For David, he knew before Solomon was born that the next son, born to him, would be the next king of Israel. However, up until his death, only Bathsheba and Nathan knew of it. Bathsheba did not advocate for Solomon to become the king, but she did remind David of his promise to her. "David, you're sick, about to die, people are assuming roles and taking positions themselves – the nation needs to know who will sit on your throne! We need you to make this transition while you are still alive!"

In David's case, his successor would be the first heir to become the next king in Israel's history. Imagine if Bathsheba was the only one who knew David's plan and had to convince everyone that David had picked her son to be the next king. To further complicate matters, Solomon was not the oldest son alive at the time, thereby not the next in line of succession, either. Thus, to ensure a smooth transition of power and that the unfinished work of building the temple would be complete, David had to order Zadok, the priest, Nathan, the prophet, and Benaiah the military commander, to coronate and consecrate Solomon as the next King of Israel.

QUESTIONS FOR REFLECTION
1. What is your biggest concern or reason for not developing a succession plan or naming a successor?
2. What can be done to address this concern?
3. On a scale of 1-5 with 5 being extremely confident: How likely could your "back-up QB" come off the bench and take your church to a "Super Bowl"?
4. What could you do now to better prepare your protege or your church for an eventual transition of leadership?
5. Is there a succession plan for every position in your church? Where else would one be essential or beneficial in your church?

CHAPTER 2
APPOINTING A PROTEGE TO LEAD THE
PEOPLE INTO PROMISE: MOSES AND JOSHUA

"MOSES MY SERVANT IS DEAD; NOW THEREFORE ARISE, GO OVER THIS JORDAN, THOU, AND ALL THIS PEOPLE, UNTO THE LAND WHICH I DO GIVE TO THEM, EVEN TO THE CHILDREN OF ISRAEL." JOSHUA 1:2

"And the LORD said unto Moses, get thee up into this mount Abarim, and see the land which I have given unto the children of Israel. And when thou hast seen it, thou also shalt be gathered unto thy people, as Aaron thy brother was gathered. For ye rebelled against my commandment in the desert of Zin, in the strife of the congregation, to sanctify me at the water before their eyes: that is the water of Meribah in Kadesh in the wilderness of Zin. And Moses spake unto the LORD, saying, Let the LORD, the God of the spirits of all flesh, set a man over the congregation, Which may go out before them, and which may go in before them, and which may lead them out, and which may bring them in; that the congregation of the LORD be not as sheep which have no shepherd.

And the LORD said unto Moses, Take thee Joshua the son of Nun, a man in whom is the spirit, and lay thine hand upon him; And set him before Eleazar the priest, and before all the congregation; and give him a charge in their sight. And thou shalt put some of thine honour upon him, that all the congregation of the children of Israel may be obedient. And he shall stand before Eleazar the priest, who shall ask counsel for him after the judgment of Urim before the LORD: at his word shall they go out, and at his word they shall come in, both he, and all the children of Israel with him, even all the congregation.

And Moses did as the LORD commanded him: and he took Joshua, and set him before Eleazar the priest, and before all the congregation: And he laid his hands upon him, and gave him a charge, as the LORD commanded by the hand of Moses."(Numbers 27:12-23 KJV)

This passage records, perhaps, one of the most successful transitions in leadership ever written! Moses is respected not only in religious groups but in secular groups as a great leader. By God's hand, Moses single-handedly destroyed Egypt and liberated a group of people out of slavery. Moses led people across the Red Sea on dry ground and ensured that the people always had water, food, clothing, and protection for 40 years while wandering in the wilderness. Moses talked to God directly, spent 40 days in a mountain with God, and received the 10 commandments. Today, the Ten Commandments and Law of Moses is considered one of the earliest and preserved civil and penal codes: landing Moses on the ring of honor in the United State Supreme Court. Moses formed a world religion and established a new nation. Now this man is at the end of his tenure as leader. If there was EVER an irreplaceable leader – Moses would qualify as THAT man! Who could ever replace MOSES! Yet even for Moses, God had a Joshua in place to lead God's people into the Promised Land.

After leading the children of Israel for 40 years, God speaks to Moses in Numbers chapter 27 to inform him that he will see the Promised Land, but not enter it, because he will soon die. Instead of questioning God or getting upset with God, Moses accepts God's judgment. Moses could have easily been angry with God or bitter with the people for not being able to enter into Canaan with the congregation. However, Moses being a caring and compassionate leader, asks God to place a leader over the people to lead them into the Promised Land.

"O Jehovah, the God of the spirits of all mankind, before I am taken away please appoint a new leader for the people, a man who will lead them into battle and care for them, so that the people of the Lord will not be as sheep without a shepherd." (Numbers 27:16-17 TLB)

Let's pause here for a minute. While one of the reasons for writing this book is to discourage procrastination in developing a succession plan, it is important that leaders operate in God's timing and in God's will. On one hand, one might argue that Moses waited until the last minute to ask God for a successor, on the other hand, one might argue that Moses did not need a successor until God advised him of his impending death. Surely Moses thought he would live long enough to cross into Canaan and perhaps retire there. However, once God revealed to Moses that he would soon die, Moses' immediate thoughts were not about himself, but about the people he had led for forty years. The Scripture does not suggest that Moses believed he was so great that he could not be replaced, but that Moses understood the magnitude of the assignment and sought God for a capable leader to complete it.

Moreover, Moses was humble enough to ask God to show him who should be the next leader. In the end, if it is God's people and God's promise, then ultimately its God's responsibility to reveal the successor, right? Rather than nepotistically appointing one of his sons, Gershom or Eleazar, or asking the congregation to vote for his successor, Moses asks God to reveal who will lead the people next. God immediately replies in verse 18 of Numbers chapter 27,

"The Lord replied, "Go and get Joshua (son of Nun), who has the Spirit in him," or as the NIV states "a man in whom is the spirit of leadership".

WHY JOSHUA?

This simple answer to why Joshua is the fact that he was one of two emissaries that returned from spying out Canaan with a positive report. While Scripture does not record the origin or reason for Moses' relationship with Joshua, there are a few places in Scripture where Joshua is mentioned assisting Moses even prior to Numbers chapter 14.

JOSHUA DEFEATS THE AMALEKITES

The Amalekites came and attacked the Israelites at Rephidim. Moses said to Joshua, "Choose some of our men and go out to fight the Amalekites. Tomorrow I will stand on top of the hill with the staff of God in my hands." So, Joshua fought the Amalekites as Moses had ordered, and Moses, Aaron and Hur went to the top of the hill.

As long as Moses held up his hands, the Israelites were winning, but whenever he lowered his hands, the Amalekites were winning. When Moses' hands grew tired, they took a stone and put it under him, and he sat on it. Aaron and Hur held his hands up—one on one side, one on the other—so that his hands remained steady till sunset.

So, Joshua overcame the Amalekite army with the sword. Then the LORD said to Moses, "Write this on a scroll as something to be remembered and make sure that Joshua hears it, because I will completely blot out the name of Amalek from under heaven."

Moses built an altar and called it The LORD is my Banner. He said, "Because hands were lifted up against the throne of the LORD, the LORD will be at war against the Amalekites from generation to generation."
(Exodus 17:8-15 NIV - emphasis added)

While Moses was able to watch and intercede to God on behalf of the children of Israel, it was Joshua's job to actually fight the Amalekites. Who has God gifted, and that you can trust, to fight while you pray? Who is able to faithfully build teams and execute your "orders", so you don't have to fulfill them yourself? Perhaps one of the biggest disqualifiers of someone becoming a successor is their inability to be trusted to carry out orders as directed. Every leader needs someone who can put out fires, resolve sticky issues, correct problems, break a sweat and get their hands dirty without the leader having to come down from the mountain every time to fight the battle themselves. A leader should not have to "clean-up" after Joshua, but rest assured that Joshua can and will get the job done.

As leaders, God has placed you on the mountain to watch and pray, to get vision and strategy, to intercede and to encourage. Who is the

Joshua that God has given you that can build a team, go in the valley, and fight until victory is achieved? A Moses may have to give Joshua a chance to see how he will respond to the assignment. Over time, given enough assignments, Moses will recognize who can be trusted as a Joshua to faithfully execute the God-given plan.

JOSHUA STANDS GUARD WHEN MOSES MEETS WITH GOD

"The LORD said to Moses, "Come up to me on the mountain and stay here, and I will give you the tablets of stone with the law and commandments I have written for their instruction."

Then Moses set out with Joshua, his aide, and Moses went up on the mountain of God. He said to the elders, "Wait here for us until we come back to you. Aaron and Hur are with you, and anyone involved in a dispute can go to them."

When Moses went up on the mountain, the cloud covered it, and the glory of the LORD settled on Mount Sinai. For six days the cloud covered the mountain, and on the seventh day the LORD called to Moses from within the cloud. To the Israelites the glory of the LORD looked like a consuming fire on top of the mountain. Then Moses entered the cloud as he went on up the mountain. And he stayed on the mountain forty days and forty nights." (Exodus 24: 12-18 NIV)

"Moses turned and went down the mountain with the two tablets of the covenant law in his hands. They were inscribed on both sides, front and back. The tablets were the work of God; the writing was the writing of God, engraved on the tablets.

When Joshua heard the noise of the people shouting, he said to Moses, "There is the sound of war in the camp." Moses replied: "It is not the sound of victory, it is not the sound of defeat; it is the sound of singing that I hear."

When Moses approached the camp and saw the calf and the dancing, his anger burned and he threw the tablets out of his hands, breaking them to pieces at the foot of the mountain. And he took the calf the people had made and burned it in the fire; then he ground it to powder, scattered it on the water and made the Israelites drink it."(Exodus 32:15-20 NIV)

"Now Moses used to take a tent and pitch it outside the camp some distance away, calling it the "tent of meeting." Anyone inquiring of the LORD would go to the tent of meeting outside the camp. And whenever Moses went out to the tent, all the people rose and stood at the entrances to their tents, watching Moses until he entered the tent. As Moses went into the tent, the pillar of cloud would come down and stay at the entrance, while the LORD spoke with Moses. Whenever the people saw the pillar of cloud standing at the entrance to the tent, they all stood and worshiped, each at the entrance to their tent. The LORD would speak to Moses face to face, as one speaks to a friend. Then Moses would return to the camp, but his young aide Joshua son of Nun did not leave the tent.(Exodus 33:7-11 NIV)

"So, Moses went out and told the people what the LORD had said. He brought together seventy of their elders and had them stand around the tent. Then the LORD came down in the cloud and spoke with him, and he took some of the power of the Spirit that was on him and put it on the seventy elders. When the Spirit rested on them, they prophesied—but did not do so again.

However, two men, whose names were Eldad and Medad, had remained in the camp. They were listed among the elders but did not go out to the tent. Yet the Spirit also rested on them, and they prophesied in the camp. A young man ran and told Moses, "Eldad and Medad are prophesying in the camp."

Joshua son of Nun, who had been Moses' aide since youth, spoke up and said, "Moses, my lord, stop them!" But Moses replied, "Are you jealous for my sake? I wish that all the LORD's people were prophets and that the LORD would put his Spirit on them!" Then Moses and the elders of Israel returned to the camp." (Numbers 11:23-28 NIV)

When examining these four passages of Scriptures together, there are several principles that can be extracted about the processes of identifying one's successor. As stated earlier, the Scriptures do not provide a detailed account of how Moses and Joshua first met. It appears to be a divine connection and lasting bond between Joshua and Moses. Perhaps Moses divinely saw potential in Joshua at an early age and drew him closer to himself as his personal assistant. Alternatively, perhaps Joshua gravitated towards the leadership skills and anointing on Moses' life after watching Moses divinely enact 10 plagues on Egypt. Could it be that your possible successor is right in front of you now, but is a child, teenager, or young adult that gravitates to you? Rather than push them away as a nuisance, God could be possibly sending you an aid that will one day help you complete your divine assignment!

It is amazing that on more than one occasion, when Moses was alone in the presence of God to receive divine instruction, that it was Joshua who guarded the door. In Exodus 24, when Moses goes up the mountain, he takes Joshua with him. While Joshua did not go all the way to the top with Moses, he stood between Moses and the people at the foot of the mountain, while Moses was in the presence of God for 40 days; this amount of trust speaks volumes about Moses' confidence in Joshua. It tells us that Joshua could be entrusted to remain in such a pivotal position, but also details Joshua's dedication to Moses to stand guard for 40 days for Moses while he "disappeared" into the mountains (Exodus 32:1).

When Moses returned to the camp and would enter the Tent of Meeting to talk to God face to face, it was Joshua who would guard the tent. Of all the people in the nation of Israel, Moses could trust Joshua to watch the door while he talked to God face-to-face. Indelibly, Joshua had to have felt the presence of God or heard the voice of God as he talked to Moses. Under Old Testament practice, if Joshua had in any way been impure, disloyal, or untrustworthy, it is very likely Joshua would have been killed by God while waiting on the mountain or standing outside the tent. Thus when God said to Moses, "Take thee Joshua the son of Nun, a man in whom is the spirit," Moses would have no reason to question, or doubt, whether or not Joshua had the spirit of God in him.

27

No doubt it was these experiences with Moses that made Joshua jealous for Moses sake. One can imagine Joshua thinking "How can these 70 elders have anything like Moses when I have personally witnessed firsthand how Moses stays in the presence of God? Moses has to instruct Joshua not to get upset on his account, but that it was a good thing if others shared in his experience with God.

JOSHUA BRINGS A POSITIVE REPORT AFTER SURVEYING CANAAN

"They returned from exploring the land after forty days. They went directly to Moses, Aaron, and the entire Israelite community in the Paran desert at Kadesh. They brought back a report to them and to the entire community and showed them the land's fruit. Then they gave their report: "We entered the land to which you sent us. It's actually full of milk and honey, and this is its fruit.

There are, however, powerful people who live in the land. The cities have huge fortifications. And we even saw the descendants of the Anakites there. The Amalekites live in the land of the arid southern plain; the Hittites, Jebusites, and Amorites live in the mountains; and the Canaanites live by the sea and along the Jordan." Now Caleb calmed the people before Moses and said, "We must go up and take possession of it, because we are more than able to do it."

But the men who went up with him said, "We can't go up against the people because they are stronger than we." They started a rumor about the land that they had explored, telling the Israelites, "The land that we crossed over to explore is a land that devours its residents. All the people we saw in it are huge men. We saw there the Nephilim (the descendants of Anak come from the Nephilim). We saw ourselves as grasshoppers, and that's how we appeared to them."

"And all the congregation lifted up their voice and cried; and the people wept that night. And all the children of Israel murmured against Moses and against Aaron: and the whole congregation said unto them, Would God that we had died in the land of Egypt! or would God we had died in this wilderness! And wherefore hath the Lord brought us unto this land, to fall by the sword, that our wives and our children should be a prey? were it not better for us to return into Egypt?

And they said one to another, let us make a captain, and let us return into Egypt. Then Moses and Aaron fell on their faces before all the assembly of the congregation of the children of Israel. And Joshua the son of Nun, and Caleb the son of Jephunneh, which were of them that searched the land, rent their clothes: And they spake unto all the company of the children of Israel, saying, The land, which we passed through to search it, is an exceeding good land. If the Lord delight in us, then he will bring us into this land, and give it us; a land which floweth with milk and honey. Only rebel not ye against the Lord, neither fear ye the people of the land; for they are bread for us: their defence is departed from them, and the Lord is with us: fear them not. But all the congregation bade stone them with stones. And the glory of the Lord appeared in the tabernacle of the congregation before all the children of Israel." (Numbers 13:25 - 14:10 KJV)

Finally, we conclude where we began with Numbers chapter 14. Joshua and Caleb are selected along with 10 others to spy out of the land of Canaan. All 12 return with the same report of the land being full of milk, honey, fruit and other inhabitants. However, 10 of the spies saw the opportunities and challenges as an insurmountable obstacle and prescription for failure and annihilation. Only days removed from the exodus, the 10 spies could only see what was against them but failed to remember WHO was for them! On the contrary, Joshua and Caleb saw the same opportunities and challenges as fulfillment of the promise of God and another opportunity for God to give the nation of Israel victory over its enemies. The 10 spies looked at the same problem and declared, "we can't" because "we saw ourselves as grasshoppers" whereas Caleb and Joshua declared, "we can" because "we are more than able to do it."

One could reasonably give the 10 spies the benefit of the doubt for giving Moses a realistic, fact-based, pragmatic assessment of the situation. Whereas Caleb and Joshua may have given Moses a more ambitious, faith-based, macho-driven assessment of the situation. The truth is, at times, a leader needs both types of people on their leadership team to make good, sound decisions.

Thus, the distinction between the two groups of spies cannot be determined by fear versus faith. However, two people can see the same situation differently. In verse 32 we read, "And they brought up an evil report of the land which they had searched unto the children of Israel." Chapter 14 continues with the children of Israel being so upset about the news that they begin to cry, wept all night, and murmured about Moses and Aaron to the point that on the next day, they were ready to replace Moses and return back to Egypt. The 10 spies had not only given a negative report, but also turned the people against their leader!

As the people were ready to stone Moses, Caleb and Joshua were willing to risk their lives to defend Moses before the people. The dispute got so ugly that God himself was willing to destroy the nation of Israel and start over with a new nation birthed from Moses. However, Moses interceded on behalf of the people and actually, got God to change His mind! God relented on destroying the nation of Israel in the wilderness but declared that none over the age of 20 could enter into the Promised Land except for Caleb and Joshua. (Side note: we often hear it preached and declared to be the Joshua generation. It is great to be Joshua, but not so great to be a part of the Joshua generation. The Joshua generation died in the wilderness. It was the children of the Joshua generation that actually entered into the Promised Land).

As a leader, think of who in your camp can see your vision, knows your heart, communicates it to others, and is willing to defend it when confronted with severe opposition? Joshua was not only loyal to his leader, but willing to risk his life to defend him. Joshua was loyal to God when he declared with confidence and courage before a rebellious people "the LORD is with us: fear them not" (Numbers 14:8 NIV). Every Moses needs a Joshua who will not only serve him, but also stand up for him in the time of opposition.

Leaders are not without flaws nor are they immune from making bad decisions. However, one of the ways to identify a "Joshua", is to simply look around and see who stood with you when everyone was against you. This is not to be confused with a blind loyalty or yes-man mentality. But every leader, at one point or another, will need someone who will go to bat for them, defend them before their critics, champion a cause, or build a consensus within an organization to support the decision of the leader.

Proverbs 17:17 says, "A friend loveth at all times, and a brother is born for adversity" or as other translations state it "born to share trouble," "proved in distress" "born for a difficult time" or "born for a time of adversity." One could easily substitute "brother" for "successor" and read "a successor is born to help in adversity".

One should note, based on this criterion, God has narrowed down all the children of Israel down to two people as potential successors to Moses: Caleb and Joshua. As this book will discuss later, a single criterion might reduce the number of candidates for successor, but not necessarily identify the actual successor.

As one continues to read Numbers chapter 14, God includes Joshua with Caleb as one of the only two adults that will ultimately enter into Canaan, yet when reading verse 24, God omits Joshua from the declaration "But my servant Caleb, because he had another spirit with him, and hath followed me fully, him will I bring into the land whereunto he went; and his seed shall possess it." We will later read in Scripture that as soon as the children of Israel crossed Jordan that Caleb claimed his mountain, but it would remain the job of Joshua to claim the entire land. Could it have been that God had picked Joshua to become Moses' successor here, however the time was not right to reveal it to either of them? This all brings us back to our initial passage, Numbers chapter 27 where God reveals to Moses that Joshua would succeed him in leading the people of Israel.

Now that God has revealed to Moses who will be his successor, what's next? One of the things you will notice about the four examples of successful succession discussed in this book follow a common pattern.

Most notably, the leader identifies his successor; makes a public declaration of the decision; holds a public ceremony transferring authority to the successor; and gives final words of wisdom, encouragement, and instruction to the successor and congregation before the leader passes away. While one may argue that Joshua was the clear and obvious choice, "a no-brainer" if you will, to lead the children of Israel next, Moses did not leave it a secret or up to chance to ensure that it happened. Nor did Moses wait until his death before he transferred the leadership mantle to Joshua.

Numbers 27:18-20, 22-23 (ICB) reads,

"So, the Lord said to Moses, "Take Joshua son of Nun. My Spirit is in him. Put your hand on him. Have him stand before Eleazar the priest and all the people. Then give him his orders as they watch. Let him share your honor. Then all the Israelites will obey him...Moses did what the Lord told him. Moses had Joshua stand before Eleazar the priest and all the people. Then Moses put his hands on him and gave him orders. This was just as the Lord had told him."

Deuteronomy 3:28 (KJV), adds further instructions for Moses towards Joshua, "But charge Joshua, and encourage him, and strengthen him: for he shall go over before this people, and he shall cause them to inherit the land which thou shalt see."

In Deuteronomy 34:5-12 (KJV) we read how Moses followed God's instructions in consecrating Joshua as the next leader of Israel and giving him a charge in front of the people,

"So, Moses the servant of the LORD died there in the land of Moab, according the word of the LORD. And he buried him in a valley in the land of Moab, over against Bethpeor: but no man knoweth of his sepulcher unto this day. And Moses was an hundred and twenty years old when he died: his eye was not dim, nor his natural force abated. And the children of Israel wept for Moses in the plains of Moab thirty days: so, the days of weeping and mourning for Moses were ended. And Joshua the son of Nun was full of the spirit of wisdom; for Moses had laid his hands upon him: and the children of Israel hearkened unto him and did as the LORD commanded

32

Moses. And there arose not a prophet since in Israel like unto Moses, whom the LORD knew face to face, In all the signs and the wonders, which the LORD sent him to do in the land of Egypt to Pharaoh, and to all his servants, and to all his land, And in all that mighty hand, and in all the great terror which Moses shewed in the sight of all Israel."

Who could ever replace Moses the emancipator, the lawgiver, author of the Torah, the founder of a nation and a religion, the voice of God to the people? Yet God prepared a Joshua to complete the assignment of leading the children of Israel into the Promised Land. No matter how great, accomplished, invincible, or irreplaceable one may think they are; understand that God can reveal a successor who can lead the people to the next dimension. The children of Israel had enough confidence in Moses to respect his decision to appoint Joshua as his successor. As a faithful servant to Moses, Joshua had earned the confidence and respect of the children of Israel to be their next leader.

Many successors lament that they missed out on the public affirmation of that decision although the leader informed them of their decision. It benefits the successor and the congregation to see the leader present, laying hands on the successor, and giving them a charge before the congregation. Moses laying his hand on Joshua before the congregation was not only symbolic, but for those who believe in the power of laying on of hands, it was an actual transferal of wisdom and anointing from Moses to Joshua. This symbolizes the succession being done by order of God, freely, without reservation, hesitation, or doubt. Moreover, Joshua does not have to deal with the stigma that he merely "assumed" or "asserted" himself as the next leader without the sanctioning of God or Moses. Again, there will be other issues in mourning the loss of one leader and transitioning to the new leader, but when doubt can be removed that God has placed the new leader in place, it empowers the leader to go forward!

God also knew that while it took a meek and humble man to lead the people out of Egypt, it would take a warrior and military tactician and strategist to lead them into Canaan. Specifically, it would take a different kind of leader to lead the children of Israel into their next phase as an emerging nation. While one's successor may share many similar characteristics, there may be a few that are different or unique; that will be necessary to lead the people in the next dimension. Similarly, the foundation of a house may be made of concrete, but the house will likely be constructed of wood, sheet rock and vinyl siding. Each stage, phase, and level of the building may require different materials in order to build a sound and lasting structure. Paul says it best in I Corinthians 3:7 (KJV) "So then neither is he that planteth anything, neither he that watereth; but God that giveth the increase."

In closing, we can glean five principles for Moses in search for Joshua who will lead the people into their destiny and next dimension. First, Joshua is willing to guard the mountain or tent so that Moses can talk to God. Second, Joshua is able to execute assignments so Moses can stay focused on his. Third, Joshua is willing to defend Moses before the people, even when Moses is not present. Fourth, Joshua is jealous for Moses and will not tolerate anyone disrespecting his leader. Fifth, Joshua is God's choice, not Moses' choice to be the next leader. Perhaps you are not in a similar position as Moses to have worked with a tried and trusted Joshua for several decades. In chapter 3, we will learn about a transition in leadership as the opposite; God selects a young and untested successor to lead the people and complete the unfinished work of their predecessor.

QUESTIONS FOR REFLECTION
1. Why do you believe God selected Joshua to be the next leader of Israel, even preferring Joshua over Caleb?
2. Which of the five (5) traits of Joshua is the most important when selecting a successor, and why?
3. When are conflicting character traits actually complementary? For example, Moses was meek and humble, but Joshua was a warrior and fighter.

4. How does a leader know when their time is up? How does a leader know when it is time for someone else to lead the people the rest of the way?
5. How can a leader, with the accomplishments of Moses, prepare the people to follow a Joshua, after their death?

CHAPTER 3
SELECTING A SON WHO WILL BUILD GOD A HOUSE:
DAVID AND SOLOMON

"THEN SAT SOLOMON UPON THE THRONE OF DAVID HIS FATHER;
AND HIS KINGDOM WAS ESTABLISHED GREATLY." I KINGS 2:12

"Adonijah was King David and Haggith's son. He was born next after Absalom. He was a very handsome man. He said, "I will be the king." So, he got chariots and horses for himself. And he got 50 men to run ahead of him. Now David had never interfered with him by questioning what he did. Adonijah talked with Joab, son of Zeruiah. He also talked with Abiathar the priest. They told him they would help him. But several men did not join Adonijah. These men were Zadok the priest, Benaiah son of Jehoiada, Nathan the prophet, Shimei, Rei and King David's special guard. Then Adonijah killed some sheep, cows and fat calves for sacrifices. He made these sacrifices at the Stone of Zoheleth near the spring, En Rogel. He invited all his brothers, the other sons of King David, to come. He invited all the rulers and leaders of Judah also. But Adonijah did not invite Nathan the prophet, Benaiah, his father's special guard or his brother Solomon.

When Nathan heard about this, he went to Bathsheba. She was the mother of Solomon. Nathan asked her, "Have you heard what Adonijah, Haggith's son, is doing? He has made himself king. And our real king, David, does not know it. Your life and the life of your son Solomon may be in danger. But I will tell you how to save yourselves. Go to King David and say to him, 'My master and king, you made a promise to me. You promised that my son Solomon would be the king after you. You said he would rule on your throne. So why has Adonijah become king?' While you are still talking to him, I will come in. I will tell the king that what you have said about Adonijah is true."

So, Bathsheba went in to see the king in his bedroom. He was now very old. Abishag, the girl from Shunam, was caring for him there. Bathsheba bowed down before the king. He asked, "What do you want?" She answered, "My master, you made a promise to me in the name of the Lord your God. You said, 'Your son Solomon will become king after me. He will rule on my throne.'

But now Adonijah has become king. And you did not know it. Adonijah has killed many cows, fat calves and sheep for sacrifices. And he has invited all your sons. He also has invited Abiathar the priest and Joab the commander of your army. But he did not invite Solomon, your son who serves you. My master and king, all the people of Israel are watching you. They are waiting for you to decide who will be king after you. As soon as you die, Solomon and I will be treated as criminals."

While Bathsheba was still talking with the king, Nathan the prophet arrived. The servants told the king, "Nathan the prophet is here." So, Nathan went to the king and bowed face down on the ground before him. Then Nathan said, "My master and king, have you said that Adonijah will be the king after you? Have you decided he will rule on your throne after you? Today he has sacrificed many cows, fat calves and sheep. And he has invited all your other sons, the commanders of the army and Abiathar the priest. Right now, they are eating and drinking with him. They are saying, 'Long live King Adonijah!' But he did not invite me, Zadok the priest, Benaiah son of Jehoiada or your son Solomon. Did you do this? We are your servants. Why didn't you tell us whom you chose to be the king after you?"

Then King David said, "Tell Bathsheba to come in!" So, she came in and stood before the king. Then the king said, "The Lord has saved me from all trouble. As surely as he lives, I make this promise to you. Today I will do what I promised you in the past. I made that promise in the name of the Lord, the God of Israel. I promised that your son Solomon would be king

38

after me. I promised he would rule on my throne after me." Then Bathsheba bowed face down on the ground before the king. She said, "Long live my master King David!"" 1 Kings 1:5-40 ICB

An entire book could probably be written about succession planning simply from this passage of Scripture. However, this chapter will highlight some of the unique aspects of the transition in leadership from King David to his son, King Solomon.

The question is not whether you have a successor, but rather the question is what role will you play in selecting and preparing that person to be the next leader. Failure to name a successor only leaves the question up to chance, debate, or someone "assuming" the role when it may never have been God's plan or the leader's desire for that person to "sit on the throne" next.

"Adonijah was King David and Haggith's son. He was born next after Absalom. He was a very handsome man. He said, "I will be the king." So, he got chariots and horses for himself. And he got 50 men to run ahead of him. Now David had never interfered with him by questioning what he did." (I Kings 1:5-6 ICB).

"And he [Adonijah] said, Thou knowest that the kingdom was mine, and that all Israel set their faces on me, that I should reign: howbeit the kingdom is turned about, and is become my brother's: for it was his from the LORD." (I Kings 2:15 KJV).

WHO KNOWS YOUR SUCCESSION PLAN?

In this passage, Adonijah, even before David is officially pronounced dead, names himself as David's successor and initiates his own enthronement ceremony. Granted, David was on his deathbed. Adonijah was David's oldest living son.[5] However, Adonijah was not the one that God chose to be the next leader of Israel. Yet, initially, David did nothing to stop Adonijah from usurping the throne. Lesson one: if a leader

---

[5] I Chronicles 3:1-2 list Adonijah as David's fourth son. Both Amnon and Absalom are dead. It is uncertain

senses that the non-selected heir is usurping authority, it is imperative for the leader to stop and make clear to everyone who will be the next leader!

Moreover, the passage illustrates an issue with succession planning when only the spouse or a few trusted members of the leader's inner circle know the leader's plans. One can derive from the Scripture passage that only Nathan, Benaiah, Bathsheba, and, maybe, Adonijah knew that Solomon was the predetermined heir to the throne.

"But Nathan the prophet, and Benaiah, and the mighty men, and Solomon his brother, he called not. Wherefore Nathan spake unto Bathsheba the mother of Solomon, saying, Hast thou not heard that Adonijah the son of Haggith doth reign, and David our lord knoweth it not?

Now therefore come, let me, I pray thee, give thee counsel, that thou mayest save thine own life, and the life of thy son Solomon. Go and get thee in unto king David, and say unto him, Didst not thou, my lord, O king, swear unto thine handmaid, saying, Assuredly Solomon thy son shall reign after me, and he shall sit upon my throne? Why then doth Adonijah reign? Behold, while thou yet talkest there with the king, I also will come in after thee, and confirm thy words." (I Kings 1:10-14 KJV).

Too often, we hear stories where only the spouse knows the heart of the leader in terms of a successor. However, it places the spouse in a difficult position to make known to the congregation the pastors plan or pick for their successor. Many may assume that the plan is untrue, inaccurate, or simply the spouse's own choice in the matter.

In instances where there is no surviving spouse or the surviving spouse is not the first spouse, it becomes even more complicated to prove the intentions of the leader to others. One of the most likely counter arguments is simply, "if that is who they wanted, why didn't they just say so when they were alive?" Thus, one of the advantages of transferring leadership while alive is to avoid one's family or inner circle declaring the leader's selection for successor after their death. Even if not stated prior to death, but recorded in a video or affidavit to be shared after their passing; in most cases, it is almost always best to hear the leaders themselves share their plan or pick for successor rather than a congregation hear it for the first time from a surrogate or a spouse.

GOD SELECTS SOLOMON TO BE KING

With David having so many sons, one has to ask the question: why did David select Solomon? A second look at First Chronicles chapter 3 lists Solomon as David's 10th son of at least 19 sons by his wives, not including children he had by concubines.[6] David makes clear, his decision to appoint Solomon as his successor was not based on birth-order, personal preference, or the people's choice, but by divine province.

"But the word of the LORD came to me, saying, Thou hast shed blood abundantly, and hast made great wars: thou shalt not build an house unto my name, because thou hast shed much blood upon the earth in my sight. Behold, a son shall be born to thee, who shall be a man of rest; and I will give him rest from all his enemies roundabout: for his name shall be Solomon, and I will give peace and quietness unto Israel in his days. He shall build an house for my name; and he shall be my son, and I will be his father; and I will establish the throne of his kingdom over Israel forever." (I King 22:8-10 KJV).

"Howbeit the LORD God of Israel chose me before all the house of my father to be king over Israel for ever: for he hath chosen Judah to be the ruler; and of the house of Judah, the house of my father; and among the sons of my father he liked me to make me king over all Israel: And of all my sons, (for the LORD hath given me many sons,) he hath chosen Solomon my son to sit upon the throne of the kingdom of the LORD over Israel. And he said unto me, Solomon thy son, he shall build my house and my courts: for I have chosen him to be my son, and I will be his father.

Moreover, I will establish his kingdom forever, if he be constant to do my commandments and my judgments, as at this day. Now therefore in the sight of all Israel the congregation of the LORD, and in the audience of

---

[6] I Chronicles 3:1-9

our God, keep and seek for all the commandments of the LORD your God: that ye may possess this good land, and leave it for an inheritance for your children after you forever." (I Chronicles 28:4-8 KJV- emphasis added)

Solomon was the first-born son to survive after God declared that David would not build the temple but would give him a son who would build it. After God pronounced his covenant over David's life, then came David's affair with Bathsheba, murder of Uriah, the death of David and Bathsheba's first child, but also, subsequently, the birth of Solomon. Upon the birth of Solomon, the prophet Nathan, named Solomon, Jedidiah or the beloved of God, affirming that Solomon would be unique amongst David's children[7].

DAVID CHOREOGRAPHED AND WITNESSED THE ENTHRONEMENT OF HIS SON

Not only did Solomon and the people hear from David's mouth that Solomon was the one selected to be the next king of Israel, but David also provided instruction for the enthronement ceremony.

"Then King David said, "Tell Zadok the priest, Nathan the prophet and Benaiah son of Jehoiada to come in here." So, they came before the king. Then the king said to them, "Take my servants with you and put my son Solomon on my own mule. Take him down to the spring called

---

[7] "I opine that the name Jedidiah was not really the name God gave to David's son, but it was rather and expression of this love for the kid transformed into a name. Interpreting directly from the original Hebrews translation, the word 'called' in the phrase "he shall be called" means qârâ, and it is interpreted; proclaimed, appointed, chosen, endowed, commissioned. Now, replacing the word 'called' in that phrase with any of the English meanings of qârâ, we'll see that God was not directly giving him the name Jedidiah, but he was rather establishing him as Jedidiah meaning the beloved of the Lord. Moreover, if we read through 1 Chronicles 22:9 behold a son shall be born to thee who shall be a man of rest; and I will give him rest from all his enemies round about: for his name shall be Solomon, and I will give peace and quietness unto Israel in his days"... From this verse we realize that the name Solomon was God's proposed name for David's son before he was born. So both names came from God, one to David the son's father, and the other to Nathan the Prophet. But Nathans' came after the child was born to express God's total love, while Davids' came before the child was born as a promise." https://ebible.com/questions/18857-why-did-david-name-his-son-solomon-when-god-said-his-name-was-to-be-jedidiah retrieved June 15, 2020.

Gihon. There Zadok the priest and Nathan the prophet should pour olive oil on him and make him king over Israel. Blow the trumpet and shout, 'Long live King Solomon!' Then come back here with him. He will sit on my throne and rule in my place. I have chosen him to be the ruler over Israel and Judah."

Benaiah son of Jehoiada answered the king, "This is good! And may your God make it happen. The Lord has always helped you, our king. Let the Lord also help Solomon. And let King Solomon be an even greater king than you." So Zadok the priest, Nathan the prophet and Benaiah son of Jehoiada went down. The Kerethites and Pelethites, the king's bodyguards, went with them. They put Solomon on King David's mule and went with him to the spring called Gihon. Zadok the priest took with him the container of olive oil from the Holy Tent. He poured the olive oil on Solomon's head to show he was the king. Then they blew the trumpet. And all the people shouted, "Long live King Solomon!" All the people followed Solomon into the city. They were playing flutes and shouting for joy. They made so much noise the ground shook."

David and the people witnessed Solomon sitting on David's mule and seated on his throne. David and the people witnessed the parade, the trumpets, and the oil poured on Solomon's head. Solomon had the blessing of the priest, Zadok, the prophet, Nathan, and Benaiah, the military commander. It was more beneficial to for the people and David to witness Solomon's enthronement than for it to happen six months following David's death. Moreover, David praised God for being able to witness the enthronement of his son Solomon,

"And moreover, the king's servants came to bless our lord king David, saying, God make the name of Solomon better than thy name, and make his throne greater than thy throne. And the king bowed himself upon the bed. And also, thus said the king, blessed be the LORD God of Israel, which hath given one to sit on my throne this day, mine eyes even seeing it". (I Kings 1:47-48 KJV – emphasis added).

IV. David Gives Solomon and the People a Final Charge

Not only was David able to witness his succession and the fulfillment of God's promise, David, like Moses to Joshua, was able to give Solomon specific instructions on how to handle the transition of leadership. David specifically told Solomon who to watch, who to bless, and upon whom to take revenge. How valuable would it be to an incoming leader to know from their predecessor who to avoid and who to remain connected.

"It was almost time for David to die. So, he talked to Solomon and gave him his last commands. David said, "My time to die is near. Be a good and strong leader. Obey everything that the Lord commands. Follow the commands he has given us. Obey all his laws and do what he told us. Obey what is written in the teachings of Moses. If you do these things, you will be successful in all you do and wherever you go. And if you obey the Lord, he will keep the promise he made to me. He promised: 'Your descendants must live as I tell them. They must have complete faith in me. If they do this, then a man from your family will always be king over the people of Israel.

"Also, you remember what Joab son of Zeruiah did to me. He killed the two commanders of Israel's armies. He killed Abner son of Ner and Amasa son of Jether. He killed them as if he and they were at war. But this was in a time of peace. He killed innocent men. And their blood got on his belt and sandals. You should punish him in the way you think is wisest. (But do not let him die peacefully of old age.)

"Be kind to the children of Barzillai of Gilead. Allow them to eat at your table. They helped me when I ran away from your brother Absalom.

"And remember, Shimei son of Gera is here with you. He is from the people of Benjamin in Bahurim. Remember he cursed me the day I went to Mahanaim. Then he came down to meet me at the Jordan River. I promised him before the Lord, 'Shimei, I will not kill you.' But you should not leave him unpunished. You are a wise man. You will know what to do to him. But you must be sure he is killed." (I Kings 2:1-9 ICB).

Further, David not only charged Solomon in private, but charged Solomon and the people, publicly,

"Then David ordered all the leaders of Israel to help his son Solomon. David said to them, "The Lord your God is with you. He has given you rest from our enemies. He helped me to defeat the people living around us. The Lord and his people are in control of this land. Now give yourself completely to obeying the Lord your God. Build the holy place of the Lord God. Build the Temple for worship to the Lord. Then bring the Ark of the Covenant with the Lord into the Temple. And bring in the holy things that belong to God." (I Chronicles 22:17-19 ICB)

David left no stone unturned[8]. In his final days he warns, encourages, and prepares Solomon and the people for the future. Everyone is left operating from the same playbook knowing the mission, vision, plan, and position in the kingdom. With everyone reading from the same script, Solomon had no choice but to succeed!

DAVID SETS SOLOMON UP TO SUCCEED

Not only did David provide Solomon with words of wisdom, instruction, and encouragement, he did all he could to position Solomon for success. In First Chronicles chapters 22-27, it is written how David organized the workers and resources to build the temple and he organized the priest and Levites as to how they would serve in the new temple once complete. [9]

"So, David gave an order for all foreigners living in Israel to be gathered together. From that group David chose stonecutters. Their job was

---

[8] One has to wonder if David ever talked to Solomon about the affair with Bathsheba. In preparing Solomon to be king, did David also prepare Solomon to be a man? When you see how Solomon allowed his wives to turn his heart away from God, it makes you wonder if David and Solomon ever had a man-to-man, father-to-son talk about life in general. How many sons have learned how to preach and pastor a church from their father but we never taught how to be a good husband or father. I digress...

[9] Nehemiah reaffirms the importance of a leader having the favor of God and of the blessing of the leader to accomplish any task. The people are more likely to rise up and build when they can see the hand of God on their life and the approval of their leader for the assignment.
Then I told them of the hand of my God which was good upon me; as also the king's words that he had spoken unto me. And they said, Let us rise up and build. So they strengthened their hands for this good work. (Nehemiah 2:18 KJV)

to cut stones to be used in building the Temple of God. David supplied a large amount of iron. It was used for making nails and hinges for the gate doors. He also supplied more bronze than could be weighed. And he supplied more cedar logs than could be counted. Much of the cedar had been brought to David by the people from Sidon and Tyre.

David said, "We should build a great Temple for the Lord. It should be famous everywhere for its greatness and beauty. But my son Solomon is young. He hasn't yet learned what he needs to know. So, I will prepare for the building of it." So, David got many of the materials ready before he died. (I Kings 22:1-5 ICB – emphasis added).

Then David gave his son Solomon the plans for building the Temple. Those plans were also for the porch around the Temple. They were for its buildings, its storerooms, its upper rooms and its inside rooms. They also were the plans for the place where the people's sins were removed. David gave him plans for everything he had in mind. David gave him plans for the courtyards around the Lord's Temple and all the rooms around it. He gave him plans for the Temple treasuries. And he gave him plans for the treasuries of the holy things used in the Temple... David said, "All these plans were written with the Lord guiding me. He helped me understand everything in the plans." (I Chronicles 28:11-12, 19 ICB)

"King David spoke to all the Israelites who were gathered. He said, "God chose my son Solomon. Solomon is young and hasn't yet learned what he needs to know. But the work is important. This palace is not for people. It is for the Lord God. I have done my best to prepare for building the Temple of God. I have given gold for the things made of gold. I have given silver for the things made of silver. I have given bronze for the things made of bronze. I have given iron for the things made of iron. I have given wood for the things made of wood. I have given onyx for the settings and turquoise. I have given gems of many different colors. I have given valuable stones and white marble. I have given much of all these things. I have already given this for the Temple. But now I am also giving my own treasures of gold and silver. I am doing this because I really want the Temple of my God to be built." (I Chronicles 29:1-3 ICB)

SOLOMON FULFILLS THE VISION GIVEN TO DAVID

Twenty years later, Solomon is able to dedicate the new temple and thus fulfill the vision given to his father, David! Upon the dedication of the temple, Solomon testified

"My father David wanted to build a temple as a place to worship the Lord, the God of Israel. But the Lord said to my father, 'David, it was good that you wanted to build a temple as a place to worship me. But you are not the one who will build the temple. Your own son will build my temple.' "Now the Lord has kept his promise. I have taken my father David's place. Now I am Israel's king. This is what the Lord promised. And I have built the Temple where the Lord, the God of Israel, will be worshiped." (II Chronicles 6:7-10 ICB)

"Solomon followed his father David's instructions. Solomon chose the groups of priests for their service. He chose the Levites to lead the praise. And they were to help the priests do their daily work. And he chose the gatekeepers by their groups to serve at each gate. This is what David, the man of God, had commanded. They obeyed all of Solomon's commands to the priests and Levites. And they obeyed his commands about the treasuries. All Solomon's work was done. Everything was done as he had said from the day the Temple of the Lord was begun until it was finished. So, the Temple was finished." (II Chronicles 8:14-16 ICB)

Ultimately, Solomon would go down in history as the wisest, wealthiest, and most successful king in Israel's history. Solomon's territory, wealth, palace, servants, peaceful reign, and wisdom were never matched again by another king of Israel. Thousands of years later, people all over the world read his writings and gather in Jerusalem to pray at the foundation of "Solomon's Temple." However, none of it would have been possible without a father like David who loved God, obeyed God, and submitted to the will of God regarding himself, his people, and his son, Solomon.

47

To wrap-up this Chapter, David provides at least six (6) principles for succession planning. First, make sure there is a plan that is known by the right people. Second, allow God, especially when there are multiple options, to speak to you regarding who should be your successor. Third, do not underestimate the value in making the transition in leadership while alive and able to witness it. Fourth, related to the third, by making the transition while alive, the leader is able to give a final charge to the successor and to the people. Furthermore, David does everything within his power to position Solomon to succeed. Finally, as a result of David applying the five principles, we see the sixth principle - a vision fulfilled! One can only imagine what God might do through you, or better yet, your successor if David's pattern is followed!

QUESTIONS FOR REFLECTION

1. Why do you think God selected Solomon from amongst all of David's children?
2. Do you currently have a succession plan? Who knows it or where it is located?
3. What charge, warning, or instruction would you give your successor?
4. Could Solomon have succeeded without the aid of David setting him up to succeed? What steps can you take now to better position your successor to succeed?
5. How can a leader prevent an "Adonijah" from usurping the throne?
6. What role should a spouse play in the succession planning process and transition in leadership?

CHAPTER 4
FINDING SOMEONE TO CATCH THE MANTLE WHEN IT FALLS: ELIJAH AND ELISHA

II Kings 2:1-18 NIV reads,

"When the LORD was about to take Elijah up to heaven in a whirlwind, Elijah and Elisha were on their way from Gilgal. Elijah said to Elisha, "Stay here; the LORD has sent me to Bethel." But Elisha said, "As surely as the LORD lives and as you live, I will not leave you." So, they went down to Bethel. The company of the prophets at Bethel came out to Elisha and asked, "Do you know that the LORD is going to take your master from you today?" "Yes, I know," Elisha replied, "so be quiet." Then Elijah said to him, "Stay here, Elisha; the LORD has sent me to Jericho." And he replied, "As surely as the LORD lives and as you live, I will not leave you." So, they went to Jericho. The company of the prophets at Jericho went up to Elisha and asked him, "Do you know that the LORD is going to take your master from you today?" "Yes, I know," he replied, "so be quiet." Then Elijah said to him, "Stay here; the LORD has sent me to the Jordan." And he replied, "As surely as the LORD lives and as you live, I will not leave you." So, the two of them walked on. Fifty men from the company of the prophets went and stood at a distance, facing the place where Elijah and Elisha had stopped at the Jordan. Elijah took his cloak, rolled it up and struck the water with it. The water divided to the right and to the left, and the two of them crossed over on dry ground. When they had crossed, Elijah said to Elisha, "Tell me, what can I do for you before I am taken from you?" "Let me inherit a double portion of your spirit," Elisha replied. "You have asked a difficult thing," Elijah said, "yet if you see me when I am taken from you, it will be yours—otherwise, it will not."

As they were walking along and talking together, suddenly a chariot of fire and horses of fire appeared and separated the two of them, Elisha saw this and cried out, "My father! My father! The chariots and horsemen of Israel!" And Elisha saw him no more. Then he took hold of his garment and tore it in two. Elisha then picked up Elijah's cloak that had fallen from him and went back and stood on the bank of the Jordan. ^{14} He took the cloak that had fallen from Elijah and struck the water with it. "Where now is the LORD, the God of Elijah?" he asked. When he struck the water, it divided to the right and to the left, and he crossed over. The company of the prophets from Jericho, who were watching, said, "The spirit of Elijah is resting on Elisha." And they went to meet him and bowed to the ground before him."

By most accounts, Elijah is considered one of, if not, the greatest prophets of all time! Standing beside Jesus on the mountain of transfiguration, when he pulled back his humanity to reveal his deity to the inner circle of his disciples, stood to others: Moses representing the law and Elijah representing the prophets. (Mathew 17:1-8)[10]. Inextricably linked to the promise of the Messiah coming to deliver Israel was the prophecy that one like Elijah would come first to prepare the way. (Matthew 17:10-13). Unlike previous leaders mentioned in the book, Moses and David, Elijah was not the leader of a nation, but the leader of a ministry, a school of prophets[11]. Elijah did not leave behind a throne but a gift, an anointing, a ministry – a mantle!

By the word of Elijah, there was no rain for three years (I Kings 17:1). It was Elijah that was fed by ravens providing him bread and meat

---

[10] Without the benefit of photos or paintings - anyone ever wondered how the disciples knew that the other two men beside Jesus were Moses and Elijah?

[11] Footnote from Hebrew-Greek Key Word Study Bible: The phrase "sons of the prophets" is a reference to the organization of those who were true, God-called prophets into schools at Gibeah and Naioth where they could be supervised by Samuel (I Sam. 10:10; 19:20). Later, there is mention made of a group of one hundred prophets, members of such a school, who were hidden by Obadiah to keep them from being executed by Jezebel (I Kgs. 18:4). The school set up in Gilgal (2 Kgs. 4:38-44) seems to indicate an atmosphere of a college where the prophets resided. In 2 Kings 6:1-4, there is an account of the building of such a school, and Elijah was the leader of this particular group.

daily (I Kings 17:2-5). Elijah, it was, who raised a widow's dead son back to life (I Kings 17:17-24). It was Elijah that provided the sacrifice that God consumed by fire in front of the prophets of Baal (I Kings 18:20-39). By the hand of Elijah, 3,000 prophets of Baal were slain (I Kings 18:40). It was Elijah that commanded fire to descend to consume the messengers of Ahaziah (II Kings 1:1-16).

Yet with all these accomplishments, it was the same Elijah who found himself one day running, hiding, and sitting under a tree, depressed and ready to end his life (I Kings 19:1-5). It was at this pivotal point in Elijah's life and ministry that God commanded Elijah to eat, rest, ignore the negative, and reconnect with His voice; it is at this time that God give Elijah a new assignment and an assistant to complete the assignment.

"All at once an angel touched him and said, "Get up and eat." He looked around, and there by his head was some bread baked over hot coals, and a jar of water. He ate and drank and then lay down again.

The angel of the LORD came back a second time and touched him and said, "Get up and eat, for the journey is too much for you." So, he got up and ate and drank. Strengthened by that food, he traveled forty days and forty nights until he reached Horeb, the mountain of God. There he went into a cave and spent the night.

The LORD said, "Go out and stand on the mountain in the presence of the LORD, for the LORD is about to pass by." Then a great and powerful wind tore the mountains apart and shattered the rocks before the LORD, but the LORD was not in the wind. After the wind there was an earthquake, but the LORD was not in the earthquake. After the earthquake came a fire, but the LORD was not in the fire. And after the fire came a gentle whisper. When Elijah heard it, he pulled his cloak over his face and went out and stood at the mouth of the cave. Then a voice said to him, "What are you doing here, Elijah?"

He replied, "I have been very zealous for the LORD God Almighty. The Israelites have rejected your covenant, torn down your altars, and put your prophets to death with the sword. I am the only one left, and now they are trying to kill me too."

The LORD said to him, "Go back the way you came, and go to the Desert of Damascus. When you get there, anoint Hazael king over Aram. Also, anoint Jehu son of Nimshi king over Israel, and anoint Elisha son of Shaphat from Abel Meholah to succeed you as prophet. Jehu will put to death any who escape the sword of Hazael, and Elisha will put to death any who escape the sword of Jehu. Yet I reserve seven thousand in Israel—all whose knees have not bowed down to Baal and whose mouths have not kissed him.

So, Elijah went from there and found Elisha son of Shaphat. He was plowing with twelve yoke of oxen, and he himself was driving the twelfth pair. Elijah went up to him and threw his cloak around him. Elisha then left his oxen and ran after Elijah. "Let me kiss my father and mother goodbye," he said, "and then I will come with you." "Go back," Elijah replied. "What have I done to you?"

So, Elisha left him and went back. He took his yoke of oxen and slaughtered them. He burned the plowing equipment to cook the meat and gave it to the people, and they ate. Then he set out to follow Elijah and became his servant."(I King 19:7-9, 11-21 NIV)

I.   Elisha Called to Help Elijah at a Pivotal Time in Ministry

Who did God send to help you in time of crisis or critical point in ministry? Not just to be a member of the congregation, but specifically to serve and assist you in your duties as a leader. This person could see you at your lowest, worst state, or bad day; and yet maintain your confidence, serve you faithfully, and retain a high regard for you and the anointing on your life. Is that person humble enough, like Elisha, to pour water on your hands to wash them?

Historians tell us that "Elisha accepted this call about four years before the death of Israel's king, Ahab. For the next seven or eight years, Elisha became Elijah's close attendant until Elijah was taken up into heaven." Years later, Elisha's initial credibility to the king as a true prophet would be based on the knowledge that Elisha had "washed the hands" of Elijah's. II Kings 3:11 (KJV) records,

"But Jehoshaphat said, is there not here a prophet of the LORD, that we may enquire of the LORD by him? And one of the kings of Israel's servants answered and said, here is Elisha the son of Shaphat, which poured water on the hands of Elijah."

While this book is intended for leaders as they prepare for succession, we note the importance of potential protégés spending time with their leader. Elisha did not serve Elijah merely to get his anointing, but because he had a reverence and respect for the anointing on Elijah's life. Moreover, Elisha represents someone that has been divinely sent to aid you in ministry and willing to "go the extra mile" to serve you.

ELISHA MAKE AN EFFORT TO SPEND TIME AND SERVE ELIJAH

Many successors wish they had taken advantage or made themselves more available to their leader while they were alive or in good health. Being a chauffeur , hanging out in the office, taking them out to lunch or dinner, or calling them on a more regular basis are greatly missed when the leader has passed away. Several notable pastors, bishops, and presiding bishops were known as the designated driver for the predecessor.

The golden nuggets, powerful testimonies, teachable moments, or divine downloads may prove to be essential in determining success. These moments are often unscripted, unplanned, off the cuff, unguarded, confidential, off the record, but profound, unforgettable, and full of wisdom. War stories, the nuances of navigating difficult situations, overcoming temptations, lessons learned from actual experience; things that cannot necessarily be taught in a class or learned from reading a book, are only gleaned from Elisha staying close enough to wash the hands of Elijah.

Moreover, the transfer of Elijah's mantle to Elisha may be done in private but is manifested in public and affirmed by others. How many successors have been anointed in hospital rooms sitting bedside by their leader before they transition? My pastor, Bishop Earley Dillard, often tells the story of how he went to the hospital to pray for his pastor, Bishop Harry C. Eggleston, on his deathbed. Rather than allowing Bishop Dillard to pray for him, Bishop Eggleston swiped away his hand and prayed for him instead. At this moment, Bishop Eggleston consecrated Bishop Dillard as the next pastor of Shiloh Way of the Cross Church. While not officially installed until June 8, 1985, Bishop Earley Dillard, with the full support of Bishop Eggleston's wife, Millie, immediately became pastor of the church on the day of Bishop Eggleston's death, November 25, 1984. Thirty-five years later, God has continued to prosper Bishop Dillard and Shiloh Way of the Cross Church.[12]

ELISHA MUST BE ALLOWED TO SEE ELIJAH'S SCARS

Oftentimes because a successor may be younger, more educated or skilled in certain areas, or coming into something already established, there is an assumption that the successor knows how to do the job and will be able to do it much better than the predecessor. What they fail to realize is that it was God's grace, wisdom, anointing, and battles fought and won by the predecessor, that makes the job look easy. People may see the fruit, but never see the struggle, the sweat, and labor that went into planting the vineyard. Even Jesus before his ascension had to show His disciples His wounds. Make sure your disciples see your scars from ministry before you transition to Glory!

Is there someone that God has shown you to be your successor, but the time to announce it or transfer the mantle is years in the future? Is that person someone who gave up everything, even their natural family, at times, to support you? Are they someone who was willing to go the extra mile to support you? Elisha was one of the prophets, in the school of prophets, but was willing to go the extra distance, beyond the others, to support Elijah. Elijah on four occasions: Gilgal, Bethel, Jericho, and Jordan

---

[12] For more information about Bishop Earley Dillard and Shiloh Way of the Cross Church, visit: www.shilohwayofthecross.org.

would tell Elisha to "stay here!" Yet at each instance, Elisha would respond, "I will not leave you!"

Apostle Paul further illustrates this principle in his closing salutations to the Book of Romans. Paul writes in Romans 16:12 (KJV), "Salute Tryphena and Tryphosa, who labour in the Lord. Salute the beloved Persis, which laboured much in the Lord" (emphasis added). While it is unclear exactly what type of work Persis did in comparison to Tryphena and Tryphosa, Paul makes a notable distinction in "labor" and "labored much" when saluting these female church workers. Moreover, he added the word "beloved" further indicating that Persis was worthy of special recognition and distinction. As a pastor, you might have many sons and daughters in ministry that serve you or labor with you. However, you will likely only have a few "Elisha" or "Persis" who will "labor much;" going over and beyond, to support and serve you in ministry. Elisha does not follow you merely to glean or take from you, but to serve and assist you until the very end!

WHAT IS THE MANTLE?

What was the mantle that Elisha received? Was it merely a cloak or garment? No, it represents Elisha inheriting a double portion of Elijah's anointing. Why a double portion? In the Bible, the double portion was the inheritance for the oldest son, or heir. If there were two sons, the property would not be divided in half. Rather, two thirds of the inheritance would go to the first born and the remaining one third to the youngest son. This is why Jacob desired Esau's birthright. As the second born twin son, he missed out by a few minutes on receiving a double portion of the inheritance from his father. Thus, when Esau sold his birthright to Jacob - he lost his right to inherit a double portion of Isaac's property.

In many cases, your Elisha will not necessarily inherit an organization, church, or leadership position, but will inherit a gift, anointing, charismata or office in the Kingdom. This may not merely be for a preacher but for a psalmist, prophet, intercessor, altar worker, teacher, administrator or creative for writing and creating books, songs, plays, or graphics. This person may even develop a similar mannerism, style, mechanics of ministry, yet be unique and not a mere replica of yourself.

Elisha got your "it" not because they merely practiced or mimicked your style, but had a divine download, impartation, or transfer of it upon their life. Not only will Elisha have your "it" but be able to do twice as much with your "it." They have been around you so long and so close that the anointing has become contagious in their life. Ironically, the transfer may be done in private, but the confirmation will be public. When Elisha received Elijah's mantle, he didn't have to tell the other prophets what had happened. However, when the other prophets saw Elisha smite the water, they exclaimed, "the spirit of Elijah is resting on Elisha" and they bowed down before him. The transfer of the mantle will be so apparent, others will have to recognize it. Elisha will not merely replicate your works but stand on your shoulders to do greater works. This person has your mantle. This person is your Elisha!

When examining the relationship between Elijah and Elisha, there are six principles of succession planning to be gleaned from this relationship. First, God picked Elisha to help Elijah and told Elijah where to find him. Second, God called Elisha to aid Elijah during a critical time in ministry, specifically, when Elijah was ready to quit. Thirdly, Elisha is willing to serve Elijah to the extent, and in close proximity, necessary to be able to pour water on Elijah's hands. Fourthly, Elisha is willing to go the extra mile, beyond the other prophets, to serve and support Elijah, even when Elijah instructs him otherwise. Lastly, Elisha will have Elijah's "it" and "it" will be obvious to others, especially those close to Elijah. Finally, Elisha will be able to go further and perform twice as many miracles than Elijah because Elisha served Elijah faithfully all the way until the very end!

QUESTIONS FOR REFLECTION
1. Why do you think Elisha was so willing to follow Elijah, initially?

2. Why do you think Elisha was willing to go further than the other prophets? Alternatively, why do you think the other prophets were not willing to "go as far" or "do as much" for Elijah?

3. For Elijah -in what ways can you now create opportunities for Elisha to spend more quality time with you to learn, grow, glean, and be trained? For Elisha - in what ways can you serve your Elijah better or make yourself more available to assist them?

4. What aspects of your gift, anointing, or ministry are manifested in others? How will you know if someone does or does not have your "it"?

5. How important should the "it-factor" be in selecting your successor?

6. Can Elisha duplicate or double Elisha's works without catching Elijah's mantle?

7. Could God have simply given Elisha his own mantle and ministry like many other Old Testament prophets without the prerequisite of serving Elijah? Why did Elisha have to serve first to obtain it while others simply receive it without any preconditions?

8. Where did Elijah receive his mantle?

9. Similar to Joshua, did Elisha fail by not transferring the mantle he received from Elijah to someone else?

10. What is the spiritual significance of the four stops: Gilgal, Bethel, Jericho, and Jordan?

CHAPTER 5
WHO WILL BE ENTRUSTED WITH THE KEYS TO THE CHURCH: JESUS AND THE DISCIPLES

"LASTING ACHIEVEMENT IS REALLY ONLY ACHIEVED IF IT CONTINUES AFTER WE'RE GONE." ~ JOHN MAXWELL

"Now after that John was put in prison, Jesus came into Galilee, preaching the gospel of the kingdom of God, And saying, The time is fulfilled, and the kingdom of God is at hand: repent ye, and believe the gospel. Now as he walked by the sea of Galilee, he saw Simon and Andrew his brother casting a net into the sea: for they were fishers. And Jesus said unto them, 'Come ye after me, and I will make you to become fishers of men.' And straightway they forsook their nets and followed him. And when he had gone a little farther thence, he saw James the son of Zebedee, and John his brother, who also were in the ship mending their nets. And straightway he called them: and they left their father Zebedee in the ship with the hired servants and went after him" (Mark 1:14-20 KJV).

"And he goeth up into a mountain, and calleth unto him whom he would: and they came unto him. And he ordained twelve, that they should be with him, and that he might send them forth to preach, And to have power to heal sicknesses, and to cast out devils: And Simon he surnamed Peter; And James the son of Zebedee, and John the brother of James; and he surnamed them Boanerges, which is, The sons of thunder: And Andrew, and Philip, and Bartholomew, and Matthew, and Thomas, and James the son of Alphaeus, and Thaddaeus, and Simon the Canaanite, And Judas Iscariot, which also betrayed him: and they went into an house" (Mark 3:13-19 KJV).

"And he called unto him the twelve, and began to send them forth by two and two; and gave them power over unclean spirits; And commanded them that they should take nothing for their journey, save a staff only; no scrip, no bread, no money in their purse: But be shod with sandals; and not put on two coats. And he said unto them, in what place soever ye enter into an house, there abide till ye depart from that place. And whosoever shall not receive you, nor hear you, when ye depart thence, shake off the dust under your feet for a testimony against them. Verily I say unto you, it shall be more tolerable for Sodom and Gomorrah in the day of judgment, than for that city. And they went out and preached that men should repent. And they cast out many devils, and anointed with oil many that were sick, and healed them" (Mark 6:7-13 KJV).

Jesus hand-selected men with diverse personalities and professions and took their raw talent and transformed them into a championship team. Jesus demonstrates that with intense training one can train a group of protégés to lead the people in a short period of time. In less than 3 years, Peter went from being a cussing fisherman to chief apostle in the Lord's church. He promised them in John 14:12 (KJV) Verily, verily, I say unto you, He that believeth on me, the works that I do shall he do also; and greater works than these shall he do; because I go unto my Father."

If you recruit, train, and properly role-model before your team; can someone emerge ready to lead? If necessary, could you turn the "keys to the church" over to them (literally and figuratively) after a short period of intense training? Is there someone in your ministry that was saved under you that has demonstrated the potential to lead? Perhaps, someone whom you have seen grow, mature, and develop, both as an individual and as a leader. Alternatively, the individual is inherently a born leader, but have never had the opportunity to lead anything in church?

Jesus gave his disciples parables, lectures, group assignments, homework, field trips, teachable moments, role-modeling, and hands on learning in order to train them. By no means were the disciples perfect. Some would argue that a few of his disciples should have been fired or terminated. The disciples were insensitive to the needs of children (Mark 10:13-16). They bickered over who would be greatest (Mark 10:35-45). The disciples could not pray with Jesus for one hour during the time of his greatest need (Mark 14:32-42). As he stood trial, they abandoned him and denied to others that they even knew him (Mark 14:66-72). As if Jesus had taught them nothing during their three years together, the disciples returned to their initial occupations after his crucifixion. To make matters worse, the disciples did not believe in the initial report of his resurrection (Mark 16:9-13).

Yet, Jesus knowing all of this about his disciples, continued to pour into them until the very end. Why? Jesus knew that he was not here to stay. Moreover, he knew that if the church was going to move forward, then his disciples would have to be trained and equipped to lead in the immediate future. Jesus understood that without the disciples, His ministry would have ended at the cross!

Yet after His resurrection, the Scripture records,

"Afterward he appeared unto the eleven as they sat at meat and upbraided them with their unbelief and hardness of heart, because they believed not them which had seen him after he was risen. And he said unto them, Go ye into all the world, and preach the gospel to every creature. He that believeth and is baptized shall be saved; but he that believeth not shall be damned. And these signs shall follow them that believe; In my name shall they cast out devils; they shall speak with new tongues; They shall take up serpents; and if they drink any deadly thing, it shall not hurt them; they shall lay hands on the sick, and they shall recover" (Mark 16:14-18 KJV).

"And they went forth, and preached everywhere, the Lord working with them, and confirming the word with signs following. Amen" (Mark 16:20). And as the saying goes, "the rest is history!"

What are some principles that can be learned from Jesus about preparing disciples? Biblically, 12 is significant because of the 12 tribes of Israel, the 12 disciples, and 12 gates to the City. The number 12 is also known for symbolizing faith, perfection, completeness, authority, divine rule, and the church. Thus, let's examine Jesus 'Top 12 List" of principles for leadership and producing quality disciples.

1. JESUS WAS A MAN OF PRAYER.

Jesus began and ended his ministry with prayer (See Matthew 4:2 and Matthew 26:36-46). The Scripture records numerous instances where Jesus would escape to be alone and to pray (Mark 6:46). Jesus prayed for strength, direction, and for his disciples (John 17:9-26).

Leaders have to be careful to avoid constantly pouring into others without stopping to take the time to refill themselves. Moreover, a leader should care about the needs of his team to cover them in prayer. Could it be that a team member is ineffective because of a personal matter that requires you to pray for them? Also, an effective leader must be attuned to the voice of God at all times. Contrary to most people's thinking, the longer one walks with God and the greater responsibility he gives to lead, the more one needs to spend time with God in prayer.

Proverbs 3:5-6 (NLT) say it this way, "Trust in the Lord with all your heart; do not depend on your own understanding. Seek his will in all you do, and he will show you which path to take." Leaders and their prayer life should be much like a seesaw. The higher God takes you, the lower you will need to go down in prayer. Surely, if Jesus had to take the time to pray, we do too!

2. JESUS TOOK ADVANTAGE OF TEACHABLE MOMENTS AND WAS WILLING TO ANSWER THE DISCIPLES' QUESTIONS REGARDLESS OF HOW "DUMB" THEY MAY HAVE SOUNDED.

Jesus would take any given conversation, situation, or image and turn it into a teachable moment for his disciples. Jesus did not wait for bible studies or leadership institutes to teach his disciples. If there was a lesson or principle to be learned at the moment, he would teach on the spot or as soon as he could get them away from the crowd (i.e. Mark 9:33-37; 10:13-16; 11:12-14, 20-21; 12:41-44; 13:2).

We often see this dynamic in sports. Great coaches do not know how to turn it off. They are always giving advice to their players. How can a person know the what, why, when, where, or how of ministry if they are never taught it? Don't assume anything. Especially, if you are dealing with a short time frame similar to Jesus . Every chance, moment, or opportunity to teach or train must be made to count. Even if it is seemingly a repeat lesson, let it be a reminder or reinforcement of what has been taught, but don't take it for granted that your disciples know what you know.

3. JESUS RESISTED TEMPTATION AND DID NOT SEEK PRAISE FOR HIMSELF.

Hebrews for 4:15 (KJV) informs us Jesus "was in all points tempted like as we are, yet without sin. Jesus was a "man" of character and integrity. As a teacher, Jesus could not hold his disciples to a higher standard than he was capable of living himself. Too often, too many leaders have the mistaken belief that they do not have to "practice what they preach." However, a pastor must not only teach holiness, but be holy!

Further, Jesus resisted the temptation to be praised and to be made a king (John 6:15). On numerous occasions Jesus instructed those whom he had healed or performed a miracle to "go and say nothing about it" (i.e. Mark 3:10-12; 8:26; John 6:15). Jesus even instructed his disciples not to reveal his true identity as the Messiah until after his resurrection (See Mark 8:27-30; 9:2-9). Not to disparage marking and branding. However, how many ministers today would have flyers, billboards, social media pages, and sponsors "sowing into their ministry" after just one of the miracles Jesus performed?

Granted, many leaders are guarded against the temptations of lust (sexual immorality) and greed (financial impropriety). However, many leaders fail to guard themselves against the spirit of pride, a lust for power, and the need to be worshipped. A leader must resist the temptation to be greedy for positions, platforms, or platitudes (See Matthew 4:1-11).

Paul described it this way, "Let this mind be in you, which was also in Christ Jesus: Who, being in the form of God, thought it not robbery to be equal with God: But made himself of no reputation, and took upon him the form of a servant, and was made in the likeness of men: And being found in fashion as a man, he humbled himself, and became obedient unto death, even the death of the cross. Wherefore God also hath highly exalted him and given him a name which is above every name" (Philippians 2:5-19 KJV - emphasis added). Take the lesson from Jesus. Don't strive to be "equal with God" or to make your own name great. Let God exalt you and let him "make your name great" (Genesis 12:2)!

4. JESUS DEMONSTRATED THAT HE HAD COMPASSION FOR THE PEOPLE.

On more than one occasion, the Scripture records that Jesus had "compassion" for a person or for the people (See Mark 6:34; 8:2; Luke 7:13). Isaiah speaking about the future Messiah said that he would be "a man of sorrow and acquainted with grief" (Isaiah 54:3). Too many leaders require unconditional love and loyalty from their followers, but have no love, compassion, or empathy for the needs of those under their care. To be a leader like Jesus, a pastor must love the people like Jesus!

Granted, a leader has to somewhat "guard themselves" from all of the plights and problems experienced by the people. Otherwise, the leader will get overwhelmed and burnt out quickly. However, to show or demonstrate little concern for employees, staff, co-workers, or members of one's congregation is tantamount to committing malpractice as a leader. Maybe in a corporate setting the only thing that matters is one's productivity. However, in a church, the leader is not just a CEO, but a shepherd that has been assigned by God to care for the people. For people to "care" about the mission, the leader must show that they "care" about the team and the people they have been assigned to serve.

5. JESUS WAS NOT AFRAID TO REBUKE HIS DISCIPLES OR CHALLENGE THEM TO DO MORE THAN WHAT THEY THOUGHT WAS POSSIBLE.

World renowned motivational speaker, Les Brown[13], once said, "people do not rise to low expectations...the problem is not that we aim too high and hit...we aim too low and miss!"

Thus, to be like Jesus, a leader must be willing to challenge and, at even times, "rebuke" a disciple. Jesus was upfront about the sacrifices required to become his disciple. His disciples would have to forsake all, suffer persecution, and take up their own cross in order to follow him (Matthew 16:24-26). Moreover, Jesus informed them that if they were not willing to "eat my flesh" or "drink my blood" that they could not be his disciples. Consequently, the Scripture records, "from that time many of his disciples went back and walked no more with him" (See John 6:53-68). Often leaders are afraid to have or expect high standards. Yes, many will not achieve them or even attempt to try them. However, God will always send a faithful few who not only embrace the challenge but excel at it!

Peter was one such disciple. Peter experienced Jesus rebuking him. Matthew 16:22-23 (NLT) records, "But Peter took him aside and began to reprimand him for saying such things. "Heaven forbid, Lord," he said. "This will never happen to you!" Jesus turned to Peter and said, "Get away from me, Satan! You are a dangerous trap to me. You are seeing things merely from a human point of view, not from God's." Today, if some people were Peter, they would resign from ministry, quit the church, and file a lawsuit against Jesus for talking to them in such a harsh manner. After being called a devil, you would think Peter would have betrayed Jesus, not Judas!   However, according to Scripture, Peter accepted the rebuke

---

[13] As one of the world's most renowned motivational speakers, Les Brown is a dynamic personality and highly-sought-after resource in business and professional circles for Fortune 500 CEOs, small business owners, non-profit and community leaders from all sectors of society looking to expand opportunity. For more information, visit - https://lesbrown.com/. Retrieved, July 18, 2020.

without contention and continued to follow Jesus. Which one of your disciples can humbly accept correction and remain faithful in serving with you?

Yet, the Scripture records that not only did Peter experience the "back hand" of Jesus, but Peter also saw the "front hand" of Jesus. It was Peter who received the invitation to come out on the sea to walk on the water with Jesus. You see, great leaders do not have high expectations merely to make life miserable or difficult for followers. Great leaders set high standards to bring out the best in people. Great leaders like Jesus enable their disciples to do things that they thought were impossible. If you are to be a leader like Jesus, don't be afraid to have high standards, challenge your disciples, and when necessary "rebuke them" in order to bring out the best in them.

6. JESUS KNEW HOW TO TAKE A BREAK AND GET REST.

Jesus was not only a man of prayer, but Jesus was also a man of rest. On several occasions after either teaching or ministering he would slip away to relax (See Mark 4:38; 6:31). Unfortunately, too many pastors work themselves into a premature grave. We've all heard pastors making statements such as "no rest for the weary," "I'd rather wear out than rust out" or "I'll rest when I die!"

While there may be some truth to these statements, it is important that leaders not only take care of their spiritual health, but also their mental, emotional, and physical health. It is difficult to minister to others when you are not well yourself. In addition to eating healthy and exercising routinely, a leader must be in tune with themselves and know when to "shut it down," "turn it off," and "get away" from it all! Otherwise, the work that the leader is rushing to complete, may not get done at all, especially if the leader is no longer around to do it. Say it with me - GET SOME REST! If God can rest on the seventh day, you can too! Undoubtedly, your spouse, family, congregation, and your body will thank you for it.

7. JESUS WAS SUBMITTED TO AUTHORITY.

Earlier we shared where Paul stated that Jesus "became obedient unto death, even the death on the cross" (Philippians 2:8). Jesus, God manifested in the flesh as the son of God, not only submitted himself to his heavenly father, but also his earthly parents. At 12 years old, Jesus was found in the temple after going missing for 3 days. Upon finding him, the Scripture says, "and he went down with them, and came to Nazareth, and was subject unto them" (Luke 2:51 KJV).

At the beginning of his earthly ministry, Jesus, who had no sin, submitted himself to water baptism by John the Baptist (See Matthew 3:13-17). Moreover, Jesus was subject to civil authority. Not only did he pay taxes (Matthew 17:27) but instructed others to "give to Caesar what belongs to Caesar" (Mark 12:17 NLT). Most humbly, Jesus even submitted himself to crucifixion by the hands of the Roman government.

As pastors and leaders there should be someone, or some entity, that we are submitted to and accountable. For a corporation it is the shareholders. For a non-profit entity it is the board of directors. For a small business or sole proprietorship, the owner must be accountable to customers and government entities. Even the President is co-equal with Congress and the Supreme Court and is ultimately accountable to the voters. Thus, the question, dear pastor, to whom are you submitted and held accountable?

For many, the Lord's church operates like a theocracy[14]. However, it should never operate as an autocracy[15]. As disciples follow a leader's example, are you able to model what it looks like to be submitted to authority? A common saying is "the apple doesn't fall far from the tree." Don't let it be that you have unaccountable, unsubmitted, and unresponsive disciples because you have been one yourself. Lead by the way that you desire others to follow you!

---

[14] Leaders are divinely appointed and guided to lead the people.

[15] A system of government by one person with absolute power.

8. JESUS WAS A SERVANT LEADER AND WAS WILLING TO WASH THE FEET OF DISCIPLES.

"So, Jesus called them together and said, "You know that the rulers in this world lord it over their people, and officials flaunt their authority over those under them. But among you it will be different. Whoever wants to be a leader among you must be your servant, and whoever wants to be first among you must be the slave of everyone else. For even the Son of Man came not to be served but to serve others and to give his life as a ransom for many" (Mark 10:42-45 NLT).

Most have heard, read books, and even studied the concept of "servant leadership." Thus, it is unnecessary to spend too much time here on the subject. However, it would be an incomplete list of Jesus' "Top-12" leadership principles without it. It is important to be reminded that leadership, especially in the church, is a privilege and not a right. No task is too big or too small for a good leader when it is necessary to get the job done.

Too often leaders in church, especially those with credentials, see their credentials as a certificate rather than as a license. A certificate is given for completion or in recognition for past accomplishments. Whereas a license is a permit or enablement to do more, or greater work, in the future. If age, health, or job duties prevent someone from serving in the same manner or magnitude, it should still be the leader's testimony that I served, I still serve, and I will not stop serving!

9. JESUS SPENT TIME WITH HIS DISCIPLES BY "BREAKING BREAD" WITH THEM.

"And it came to pass that, as Jesus sat at meat in his house, many publicans and sinners sat also together with Jesus and his disciples: for there were many, and they followed him. And when the scribes and Pharisees saw him eat with publicans and sinners, they said unto his disciples, how is it that he eateth and drinketh with publicans and sinners. When Jesus heard it, he saith unto them, They that are whole have no need

68

of the physician, but they that are sick: I came not to call the righteous, but sinners to repentance" (Mark 2:15-17 KJV).

Jesus not only ate the sacred Last Supper with his disciples but was notorious for eating meals with those who were labeled as "publicans and sinners." The members of the early church were known for fellowship and "breaking bread from house to house." As a pastor, how often do you share a meal with your disciples or members of your congregation? Not just business meetings over lunch; but time spent just to know more about the people you work with and serve. It's hard, if not impossible, to effectively lead, work with, or serve people whom you do not know that well. Share a meal or cup of coffee sometimes with your disciples and watch it make a difference in your life and ministry.

10. JESUS UNDERSTOOD THE POWER OF EFFECTIVE DELEGATION.

An entire chapter of this book could be written on the power of effective delegation. If anyone could have done it all by himself, it would have been Jesus. Yet Jesus not only called the 12 disciples to be his followers, but an additional 70 to aid in the ministry. Jesus commissioned them to go out to preach, heal the sick, and to cast out demons. Jesus not only gave them a charge, but he also provided them with the training, staff (he sent them out two-by-two) and the endowment or power to get the job done.

For delegation to be effective, it requires trust, communication, and accountability. What is the overall mission? What is the specific assignment? What resources are needed (i.e. training, money, equipment, staff, etc.)? What is the deadline? What are the risks, consequences, or repercussions if things are not done by the deadline or to a sufficient quality?

One of the greatest biblical examples of one who implemented an effective delegation system was Moses. In reading Exodus 18:17-25, Moses was overwhelmed with the task of judging the people. Moreover,

69

the people were becoming impatient and dissatisfied. Jethro, Moses' father-in-law, conveys to Moses that "the work is too heavy for you, you cannot handle it alone." Moreover, Jethro implores Moses to (1) "select capable" and "trustworthy men," (2) "appoint them," (3) "teach them" and (4) let them handle the "simple cases." Jethro further advises Moses that if he does so it will "make your load lighter," "you will be able to stand the strain," and the "people will go home satisfied." If Moses, the great emancipator, author of the Pentateuch, and one who stood in the presence of God and talked to God directly had to learn how to delegate effectively, we must learn to do so likewise.

Will disciples and delegates get it wrong sometimes? Yes. However, without an opportunity, they will never have a chance to get it right! The Scripture records, "And the seventy returned again with joy, saying, Lord, even the devils are subject unto us through thy name" (Luke 10:17 KJV). With effective delegation, not only can the team share in the work, but also share in the success. Your strain will be lessened, and the people will be more satisfied.

11. JESUS BUILT A TEAM WITH DIVERSITY, INCLUDING HAVING A JUDAS ON IT.

Granted, all of Jesus' 12 disciples were Jewish men. However, the Scripture does not record where any of his disciples shared in his profession (carpenter), grew up in the same town (Nazareth), or came from the religious leadership (priest, Levites, etc.)

Too often leaders adopt the fallacy that in order to achieve unity a team must have unanimity. However, great leaders appreciate collaboration, diversity of thought, and the ability of a team to take a good idea and make it a great idea. A team consisting of only "yes men" or monolithic thinking will never achieve its maximum potential. Jesus took "fisherman" and made them "fishers of men" (Mark 1:16-17). A great leader like Jesus is able to take the diverse and unique experiences, talents, and skills and redirect them towards a common goal or mission.

70

Beware, great leaders at some point in their tenure will have a Judas on the team. Someone who will betray you, sell you out, and seek to have you destroyed. As Elder Mark Moore, Jr once shared in a "Branding Like Jesus" master class, "You can't be Jesus without a Judas!" Yet, for God's servant a Judas can do no more to a leader than what God allows. Often God will use a "Judas", not to destroy you, but to propel you closer to your destiny. "And we know that God causes all things to work together for good to those who love God, to those who are called according to *His* purpose" (Romans 8:28 NASB). Moreover, don't allow the negative experience from a disciple like Judas to cause you to have a jaded perspective or to miss out on the eleven "ride or die" disciples who will stick with you until the very end.

12. JESUS WAS WILLING TO "LAY IT ALL ON THE LINE" FOR THE CAUSE.

"I am the good shepherd: the good shepherd giveth his life for the sheep... As the Father knoweth me, even so know I the Father: and I lay down my life for the sheep...No man taketh it from me, but I lay it down of myself. I have power to lay it down, and I have power to take it again..." (John 10:11,15, 18 KJV).

A leader cannot demand more from their team than what they are willing to sacrifice themselves. Jesus could demand the most from his disciples because he sacrificed the most for the church. Pastors should lead by giving their time, talent, and treasure to the ministry. No leader should expect its team members to have a greater commitment or dedication to the mission, vision, or the team itself, than the leader.

A leader should be able to say, "I'm not requiring you to do more than I am willing to do myself." By experiencing the beating and tortuous death of the cross, Jesus demonstrated to his disciples that he was in fact willing to "go the distance," "lay it on the line," and "leave everything on the field". As a result, the disciples had no choice, but to follow suit and endure persecution, beatings, incarceration, and ultimately death for the "cause of

71

Christ" (Philippians 1:13, Philemon 1:23). Because of the sacrifice Jesus made at Calvary, we have salvation. But it is because of the sacrifices made by the disciples and early Christians that we have a church!

CLOSING

Question to ponder: If after praying for 40 days to select his team, providing 3 years of personal training, mentorship and master classes, and had not anyone on that team capable to lead next, would that have been the fault of Jesus or the disciples? If Jesus, God in flesh, can be beaten mercilessly and crucified on a cross; literally purchasing the church with his own blood, sweat, and tears, can turnover HIS church to someone else - if Jesus can, surely you can, too!

QUESTIONS FOR REFLECTION

1. How do you assess potential? How can a leader know that a "Simon" has the potential and capacity to become a "Peter"?
2. Of all the men that were in the area at the time, why did you think Jesus picked the 12 men that he selected to be his disciples?
3. Jesus had 12 disciples but 3 of the 12 were considered to be in his "inner circle." What do you think qualified them to have this special access to Jesus? Is it okay for a leader to have an "inner circle" from within their group of disciples?
4. Why do you think Jesus did not have anyone from his family or from the religious community as one of his 12 disciples?
5. Who was more essential to Jesus in him fulfilling his purpose - Judas or Peter?

CHAPTER 6
ADDITIONAL CHARACTERISTICS OF A SUCCESSOR

After examining the relationships of Moses and Joshua, David and Solomon, Elijah and Elisha, and Jesus and the Twelve Disciples, this chapter will discuss ten additional characteristics for a potential successor. The list is not exhaustive or any particular rank or order. Some may be more important to others, applicable to all, or not a major criterion in selecting a successor. In Appendix B there is a Successor Evaluation designed to help leaders identify and train potential successors.

AGE

Age ain't nothing, but a number, right? We have all met both wise youth and old fools. The Bible gives us both ends of the spectrum for successful leaders: Josiah at age 8 when he becomes king of Judah and Joshua at age 83 when he takes the helm from Moses to lead the children of Israel into the Promised Land. Our history books are filled with numerous examples of how some of the greatest businesses as well as religious, civil and political movements were led by individuals in the late teens and early 20's when they got started. Should age even be a factor? Is it even legal for a church to consider one's age in selecting a pastor?[16] Age like other

---

[16] Under federal law, and most state law, under the religious exemption, churches and clergy are exempt from various employment discrimination laws, including age. Thus if church doctrine or rule mandated that a pastor retire at age 80, in most jurisdictions, it would be upheld and not viewed as age or employment discrimination. However, in a different profession, such as with an 80-year-old partner in a law firm, the same requirement would likely violate

characteristics is not determinative but should be taken into consideration. What are the ages of the prospective successors? What is the physical health of the potential successors?

It is true that no one knows how long anyone will live, but if a person has reached a certain age and degree of health, the question must be asked: are they the future for this church? The answer could be maybe so! This person could be the future or a transitional leader. The role of the transitional leader is to give more time for God to prepare the ultimate successor. If the leader has left a big shadow or large shoes to fill, who is eager or equipped to be the one to fill them?

BISHOP R.C. LAWSON | BISHOP H.C. BROOKS | BISHOP C.H. MASON

The following are three examples of transitional leaders who bridged the gap between the founder of the movement and the ultimate successor. First example, in the Church of our Lord Jesus Christ of the Apostolic Faith, Inc. after the passing of its founder, Bishop R.C. Lawson in 1961, Apostle Hubert J. Spencer was elected as presiding bishop and served from 1961-1973. In 1973, Apostle William L. Bonner became the leader of COOLJC and served as presiding bishop and later as chief apostle for the next 42 years, until his death in 2015. During his tenure, Bishop Bonner would simultaneously pastor five churches in five states, found a bible college, establish a board of apostles, extend COOLJC's imprint around the globe, and oversee an exponential growth in the number of churches to become a part of the organization.

Second example, in 1967, Bishop Henry C. Brooks, founder of The Way of the Cross Church of Christ, International passed away unexpectedly after serving as founder and pastor of the "Mother Church" for 40 years and

---

the Age Discrimination Act. In the case of the law firm, it may develop a job description that requires partners to work 50 hours a week. Under that requirement an 80 year-old may or may not be able to or desire to work that many hours per week. Yet the decision would be based on individual ability and not on an arbitrary maximum age rule.

presiding bishop of the organization for 34 years[17]. At the time, his son, Alphonzo D. Brooks had acknowledged his call to ministry, but had not given his initial trial sermon. After a period of rotating ministers on an interim basis, the church split. As a result, Bishop H.C. Brooks' cousin, Bishop J.L. Brooks, moved from North Carolina to Washington, DC to pastor the church. After pastoring the church for 10 years, Bishop J.L. Brooks turned the church over to then, Elder Alphonzo D. Brooks, who would pastor the church for the next 40 years and now serves as the presiding bishop of The Way of the Cross Church of Christ International. In 2017, on the 90th church anniversary, The Way of the Cross (Mother) Church moved into a brand new, state of the art, 1,600 seat facility in Capitol Heights, Maryland.

Third example, after founding and leading the Church of God in Christ for 54 years, Bishop C.H. Mason passed away in 1961. For the next seven years, COGIC was led by Bishop O.T. Jones. After lawsuits and elections, in 1968, Bishop J.O. Patterson was elected presiding bishop and would serve in that capacity for the next 21 years; the longest in history to serve as an elected presiding bishop of COGIC. Today, COGIC is the largest predominantly African American Pentecostal denomination in the United States.

These examples are to demonstrate how it might be best to have someone else "wear the shoes" of a beloved establishmentarian for a season, to give more time for the "shoe size" of the ultimate successor to grow. Someone who has more maturity, wisdom and experience--coupled with a resume of seniority and service within the organization, might be best suited to handle the difficult and complex transitional season of leadership. Otherwise, it might be a very awkward, clumsy and even a perilous situation for the future leader and the church.

---

[17] Bishop R.C. Lawson ordain Bishop H.C. Brooks as an elder and chartered The Way of the Cross Church of Christ in 1927 as a part of the Church of Our Lord Jesus Christ of the Apostolic Faith, Inc. In 1933, Bishop H.C. Brooks and The Way of the Cross Church became an independent entity.

However, when considering the age of a prospective successor, let's not ignore the fact that failure to enthrone a Josiah at the age 8 could mean that Israel would miss out on having one of the greatest kings ever. II Kings 23:25 (NIV) records, "Neither before nor after Josiah was there a king like him who turned to the LORD as he did—with all his heart and with all his soul and with all his strength, in accordance with all the Law of Moses."

At the age of 16, Josiah instituted much needed reforms that purged the land of idolatry, restored the temple, reinstituted the celebration of the Passover, renewed covenant, and ignited revival in the land. Ultimately, this eight-year-old would lead Judah for thirty-one years before being killed in battle. "He did what was right in the eyes of the LORD and followed completely the ways of his father David, not turning aside to the right or to the left." (II Kings 23:2 NIV) Not only was Josiah right in the eyes of the Lord, but he was also the right man for the job! Don't disqualify Josiah because you think he is too young to fill your shoes, when in fact it might be best if he walks in his own shoes!

Lovers of history will appreciate this. What if, then Senator, Barack Obama had heeded the voices of his critics and waited another four years before running for president? Would we have had our nation's first African American president? What if A. Phillip Randolph, visionary and organizer of the 1963 March on Washington had not been willing to give voice to a 34-year-old Martin Luther King; would we have heard about a dream that would transform a nation? Even to appreciate this more, one would have to go back further in time to know that if the pastors in Montgomery, Alabama had not given a new, up and coming, 26 year old pastor from Atlanta the opportunity to lead the successful Montgomery Bus Boycott; the world may not have heard of a Rev. Dr. Martin Luther King, Jr. [18]The key

---

[18] We would be remiss if we did not acknowledge the youngest speaker at the March on Washington: The Honorable John Lewis (1940 - 2020). As a college student, Lewis was a leader of the Student Nonviolent Coordinating Committee

to enjoying any good fruit or vegetable is knowing when it is ripe and ready to be consumed. Why make a successor wait or forfeit their turn when they are ready to lead now? Don't be guilty of letting good fruit spoil or go to waste because they are left sitting in the basket too long! This could be their season, their moment in time, to make a lasting change and leave their indelible mark on history.

VISION

Proverbs 28:19 (KJV) says, "where there is no vision, the people perish; but he that keepeth the law, happy is he." The Expanded Bible (EXB) gives more clarity to how dangerous it is for the people, when there is a lack of vision. The EXB says it this way, "where there is no word from God [vision; prophecy], people are uncontrolled [the people perish], but those who obey what they have been taught [guard the law] are happy [blessed]. Habakkuk expands upon this further, when he writes,

"And the LORD answered me, and said, Write the vision, and make it plain upon tables, that he may run that readeth it. For the vision is yet for an appointed time, but at the end it shall speak, and not lie: though it tarry, wait for it; because it will surely come, it will not tarry." Habakkuk 2:2-3 (KJV).

When these Scriptures are viewed in conjunction, one can glean at least five principles as it relates to succession planning: (1) have a vision (2) write it down (3) make it plain (4) know the appointed time; otherwise,

---

(SNCC) which organized sit-ins and bus boycotts. At age 21, Lewis became one of the 13 original Freedom Riders working with CORE (Congress of Racial Equality). At age 23, recognized as the leader of one of the "Big Six" civil rights organizations, Lewis was a featured speaker at the historic march. While still in his mid-twenties, Lewis would coordinate the "Mississippi Freedom Summer" to register black voters in the South. In 1965 Lewis was brutally beaten, with his skull fractured, as a participant in the "Bloody Sunday" Selma March. The widely televised march compelled President Lyndon Johnson to seek and eventually sign the Voting Rights Act of 1965. Lewis would go on to serve in the United State Congress from 1986 until his passing from pancreatic cancer on July 17, 2020.

(5) the people will perish or act out of control. Do you have a vision for your church? Has it been documented in writing or captured in a visual rendering of it? Do members of your congregation know it? What about your leadership team? Have you ever shared your vision with your potential successor? If not, the Scripture warns us that the people will act out of control and ultimately perish.

The fifth principle from this passage is that the vision is for an "appointed time" or as the GNB translates it, "put it in writing, because it is not yet time for it to come true. But the time is coming quickly, and what I show you will come true." What if God gives you a vision that is set to come to pass during the tenure of the next leader? While it is be important for a successor to hear from God and develop their own vision, a leader should consider who knows their vision, shares that vision for the ministry, and is capable of fulfilling that vision. Can they see what you see, embrace it, and make it better? What if the disciples disobeyed Jesus and not tarried in the upper room until they were endowed with power from on high? Imagine if Joshua decided to reroute the Israelites back to Egypt after Moses died? What if Solomon discarded David's plans to build a temple? What made it difficult if not impossible for the successor to deviate from the vision, was the fact that the successor and the people knew the vision!

Further, has the protégé ever demonstrated the ability to create and cast a vision? Meaning, are they over a ministry or auxiliary within a church but never initiate any new ideas for that ministry? As a pastor, you may have placed this individual over the youth ministry sharing with them your overall vision, goals, objectives for the ministry but left the actual creation and developing of ideas, plans, and programs to the leader. Months go by, you ask them what have they come up with, and they have nothing! Not only should they have conceived an idea by now but even been proactive in presenting it to the leader. An individual who has not developed the ability to see, may be a good team member, but unfortunately, may be too blind to become the actual leader.

LEADERSHIP AND ADMINISTRATIVE ABILITIES

Henry Ford once said "vision without execution is just hallucination." Joel A. Baker expands further on this principle stating, "vision without action is merely a dream. Action without vision just passes the time. Vision with action can change the world." Yes, a good leader must have integrity, passion, charisma and good communication skills. Yet, in many ways, none of these things matter, if ultimately the individual can't get the job done! A pastor must have management and people skills, and emotional intelligence in order to be successful. A protégé can be a nice person, a good speaker, and overall a highly anointed individual, but the question is can they get the job done?

Even if this person has a great team around them and the willingness to delegate duties to others, if that person consistently lacks focus or the ability to provide broad-based guidance to the organization, it will fail. Alternatively, if a person is hard to get along with, or hard to work with; then they will not be successful, either. Unquestionably, there are different leadership styles and methods, and your successor may not have the same as yours. However, the question is less about "how" they lead, but "can" they lead? Joshua was a different leader than Moses. However, Joshua had a record of leading the people into battle and on to victory. Moses could die in peace knowing that Joshua could get the job done because Joshua had a record of performance and completing assigned tasks while Moses was alive.

DOCTRINE

Doctrine (from Latin: doctrina, meaning "teaching" or "instruction") is a codification of beliefs or a body of teachings or instructions, taught principles or positions, as the essence of teachings in a given branch of knowledge or in a belief system[19]. Luke records in the Book of the Acts of the Apostles that the early church "...continued steadfastly in

---

[19] https://en.wikipedia.org/wiki/Doctrine. Retrieved May 27, 2020.

79

the apostles' doctrine and fellowship, and in breaking of bread, and in prayers."

Thus, four sets of questions can be derived from this Scripture: (1) Can someone from a different church, reformation, or denomination be a viable candidate for succession? (2) How well do you know what your potential successor actually believes? Are you assuming that their beliefs are identical to yours? (3) Do you know if your successor will continue steadfastly in your doctrine? Does that, should that, even matter to you? (4) Are their aspects of your church doctrine or tradition that you want to change but are hesitant or reluctant to change? Are you hoping or anticipating that your successor will do it so that you do not have to make the change during your tenure? Should you make the change during your tenure so that your successor does not have to make the change during their administration?

Much of Paul's letters were written to correct erroneous doctrine or false teaching that were given to his congregations by false prophets and teachers. Paul marveling at this reality writes to his church in Galatia "But though we, or an angel from heaven, preach any other gospel unto you than that which we have preached unto you, let him be accursed" (Galatians 1:8 KJV). He warns his son Timothy, "For the time will come when they will not endure sound doctrine; but after their own lusts shall they heap to themselves teachers, having itching ears; And they shall turn away their ears from the truth, and shall be turned unto fables." (II Timothy 4:3-4 KJV).

The Bible gives numerous examples where one king was righteous, and the next king was unrighteous. Not to suggest that a modification in beliefs is on the same level but introducing a doctrine that is in stark contrast to the predecessor may impact the people in similar ways. In the Bible, the people did not know what to believe and as a result, they embraced or developed their own ideologies and doctrines. In the book of Judges, it says, "everyone did what was right in their own eyes." For a congregation, like any human, a radical change in diet can cause severe digestive problems or regurgitation if not administered properly.

A successor might have different preferences or priorities, but fundamentally, will they adhere to the same belief system as you? Not to suggest that a successor should be a clone of yours, but neither should they have beliefs radically different or diametrically opposed to yours, either. Yes, the method may change, but the message of the gospel should essentially remain the same. The sons of Issachar were known for "discerning the times." Thus, a leader should know what is negotiable and non-negotiable in their doctrine. Will the successor introduce new, unsound, or a perverted doctrine? Will this doctrine undo or negate everything you have established, taught, and upheld during your tenure as pastor?

Even if there is a necessary and God-ordained shift in philosophy or approach to ministry; will the next person operate with a level of respect for the predecessor and a certain level of sensitivity to the congregation? Will the approach towards change be more in the form of reviling the predecessor or bringing further revelation to a premise? Naturally, sons will do things different than their fathers, but a son should never disrespect their father in the process. It is possible to build upon, without tearing down; and a successor must be able to understand and navigate the difference.

BISHOP PAUL SILVESTER MORTON[20]

After moving to New Orleans and becoming a member of the church three years prior, Paul S. Morton, was elected the next pastor Greater Saint Stephens Missionary Baptist Church in New Orleans, Louisiana, after the sudden and unexpected death of its pastor. Only 25 years old at the time, still single, and having been raised his entire life in the Church of God in Christ, Morton had earned the love and respect of the congregation.

---

[20] For more information about the life and ministry of Bishop Morton, I recommend reading his autobiography, Changing Forward © 2012, Abingdon Press.

Soon after becoming the pastor, Greater Saint Stephens grew from 647 members to over 20,000 members presently and expanded to three church locations in the Greater New Orleans area. In 1993, Morton co-founded the Full Gospel Baptist Fellowship International, bridging the gap between Pentecostals and Baptists. Since its inception, Full Gospel has grown to over one million members, from five thousand congregations, and dozens of countries around the globe.

In 2005, following an unanticipated temporary relocation to Atlanta, as a result of Hurricane Katrina, Morton would establish Changing a Generation Full Gospel Baptist Church. This change made Morton not only the pastor of one church in three locations but one church in two different states. In 2013, Bishop Morton retired as presiding bishop of Full Gospel and named Bishop Joseph Walker of Nashville, Tennessee, as his successor. In 2019, Morton announced his retirement as pastor of Changing a Generation FGBC. Morton plans to install his successor as pastor after allowing his successor to shadow him daily for the next twelve months[21].

A highly sought-after speaker, singer, author, and transformational leader, Bishop Paul S. Morton, Sr., will undoubtedly go down in history as one of the most influential and impactful Christian leaders of the 20th and 21st Centuries.

CHARACTER AND "COACHABILITY"[22]

---

[21] Due to the unprecedented season caused by Covid-19, Bishop Morton in June 2020 announced a delay in his retirement to help guide the church through the pandemic.

[22] This section is not written to judge or condemn anyone. John 3:17 says "For God sent not his Son into the world to condemn the world; but that the world through him might be saved." However it does suggest that for one to serve in leadership, at the pastoral level, the individual should be an example to the congregation and have reached a certain level of spiritual maturity. Isaiah gives us the solution when he found himself in a similar situation, *"Then said I, Woe is me! for I am undone; because I am a man of unclean lips, and I dwell in the midst of a people of unclean lips: for mine eyes have seen the King, the LORD of hosts. Then flew one of the seraphims unto me, having a live coal in his hand, which he had taken with the tongs from off the altar: And he laid it upon my mouth, and*

"After this thing Jeroboam returned not from his evil way but made again of the lowest of the people priests of the high places: whosoever would, he consecrated him, and he became one of the priests of the high places." (I Kings 13:33 KJV)

It's been often said, "don't let success take you where your character can't sustain you!"   As discussed further in Chapter 8, God disqualified Eli's sons and Samuel's sons from being the successor to their father because of their lack of character and integrity. David's tenure as king was plagued with family problems because of his illicit affair with Bathsheba.   Paul, in his letters to Timothy and Titus gives detailed qualifications regarding morality, character, and reputation for a person to serve in church leadership.

As a pastor you might be privy to information about a possible successor, that is unknown to the congregation, but is in fact a disqualifier for that person to become the next leader, at least for now. You might have a Sampson, highly anointed but undisciplined and repeatedly makes poor decisions that undermine their potential.[23] This is not to judge or condemn anyone or suggest that God cannot forgive a person or use someone in the future.   However, it would be unwise to put that person in charge prematurely knowing that the individual still has "major" issues that they are working through. To put an injured quarterback back in the game, when injured or recovering from an injury, not only places the quarterback at risk

---

said, Lo, this hath touched thy lips; and thine iniquity is taken away, and thy sin purged. Also I heard the voice of the Lord, saying, Whom shall I send, and who will go for us? Then said I, Here am I; send me. And he said, Go, and tell this people, Hear ye indeed, but understand not; and see ye indeed, but perceive not." If you are "unclean;" stay on the altar a little longer. That is where the Lord can touch you and purge you. Ultimately, God can release you to "go and tell" His people and help them to understand Him.

[23] Some would argue that Sampson fulfilled his assignment by serving as judge for 20 years and in his death, prevailing over the Philistines. But this does not negate the fact that Sampson died as a tragic figure due to his lack of disciplined and poor decision-making. See Judges Chapters 13-16 for more on the life of Sampson.

for permanent disability, but also can create a precarious situation for the entire team.

It is true that nobody is perfect. However, even if saved, somehow the potential successor is still dealing with immoral addictions, questionable tendencies, or anger management issues; they may not be the ideal candidate for pastor at the moment. If an individual is dealing with a season of severe marital issues, mental health challenges, or grief; then they may need more time to sort through those matters before they become a pastor. Perhaps someone who is recently divorced, had an affair, bore a child out of wedlock, or in general, is "single and stumbling," could benefit from having more time to be strengthened and restored. In today's world, even from a legal standpoint, one has to even consider if the person has good credit, could pass a background check, or has a pattern of poor financial stewardship, or criminal record. Further, should someone who has the means, but is unwilling to support the church financially, or on a consistent basis, be a successor?

This potential successor may need more time for counseling, healing, teaching or maturing before having the pressure of pastoring thrust upon them prematurely. Especially, in the social media age, the stress and weight of ministry, the elevated platform and visibility of being a pastor, and the heat and illumination from the bright lights on the "big stage", can not only expose, but exasperate those issues. If not treated properly these "issues" can potentially retard recovery or even be in some way fatal to the individual. Often the determining factor in this regard is whether the person is repentant, teachable and willing to grow from it. Once again, the question may not be a matter of "never", but it might be a "not now" type of situation.

For five weeks during the spring of 2020, sports fans from around the globe were enthralled with ESPN documentary series, *The Last Dance*. *The Last Dance* told the story of Michael Jordan and the Chicago Bulls dynastic pursuit of six championships in the 1990's. Many watched with a greater appreciation of the mental toughness and the drive-to-win of Michael Jordan. Most sports fans and historians, almost unanimously,

84

name Michael Jordan as one of the greatest basketball players of all time. However, raw talent, discipline, and drive alone, was insufficient for Michael Jordan to win any championships. It took Michael Jordan being introduced to coach, Phil Jackson, and buying into Phil Jackson's team philosophy and triangle offense. And as you know, the rest is history. Jordan had such loyalty, respect and appreciation for Jackson that when the Bulls decided not to renew Phil Jackson's contract, Jordan decided to retire from the team.

Albeit gifted and highly anointed, a protégé must be humble and submissive enough to a leader to be trained, coached, and even disciplined, in order to grow and improve as a "player". Bishop Mark A. Moore, Sr. in his book, *Provisions for the Journey*, captures and expresses this fundamental truth clearly when he says,

"Most Christians want to go for God, but few want to grow for Him. And yet fulfilling the call of God always requires growth, which makes most of us uncomfortable. Our problem with growth is this – it necessitates change. We tend to hate most changes not initiated by us. We long to change the world without ourselves being changed. We want God to douse us with spiritual "Miracle-Gro" so that we sprout up into greatness without going through any of the normal painful processes that accompany spiritual growth. Sorry to be the one to break this to you, but it won't happen. In order to grow, you are going to have to do the fundamentals: start with the "sincere milk" of the Word; advance on to "spiritual meat;" submit to spiritual authority; accept reproof and correction, and prove yourself faithful in service. Your growth trajectory is determined by your willingness to change". [24]

Without the championship rings, Jordan would have gone down in history as a good, maybe even a great player, but definitely not as the best player ever! It took Phil Jackson, and the willingness of Michael Jordan to be coached by Phil Jackson, to make Michael Jordan and the Chicago Bulls

---

[24] Provisions for the Journey by Bishop Mark A. Moore, Sr. © 2017 Keen Vision Publishing, Day 29, "Send Me...I'll Grow"

of the 1990's one of the greatest dynasties ever, and Michael Jordan one of the greatest athletes of all time!

TRUSTWORTHY

William Shakespeare once said, "Love all, trust a few, do wrong to none." Can you trust a potential successor with sensitive, privileged, private, or confidential information? Will their spouses, family members or others in the congregation know your thoughts, plans, and ideas before they are finalized? Can matters be discussed and debated without it being leaked outside of the room? Even if there was vigorous and robust debate in a meeting, are they capable of leaving the room speaking the same thing, even if they disagreed?

Can you trust them with money, trust them around members, or trust them to "be in charge" when you are absent? Like David, no leader can withstand an Absalom constantly critiquing their decisions behind their back. Neither, like Jesus, does a leader need a Judas, who after a disagreement will turn them over to their enemies. Judas will eat dinner with you, kiss you on your cheek; yet betray you in private, sell you out, and set a trap for you to fail! Contrastingly, Jesus also had a trusted inner circle that he could safely pull back humanity and reveal His divinity. Likewise, pastors need a trusted inner circle that they can pull back their glory and reveal their humanity. If your protégé is not a trusted member of your inner circle or core team, then they very well may not be suitable to be a successor.

RELIABLE AND DEPENDABLE

Whereas reliability and dependability are akin to each other they are slightly different. A dependable person means that they can be trusted, be faithful, and will show up when needed or called upon. Whereas, a reliable person can be called upon to get the job done correctly or with skill. A dependable person has consistency, but a reliable person has competency. For instance, a plumber can be reliable, but not dependable. Meaning, they are good at what they do, (reliable), but will they show up when I call them,(dependable)? Understandably, sometimes in church we place priority in dependability over reliability. We have to work with who shows up consistently, not because they are the best, but because they are the most faithful. Jesus said, "well done, good and faithful servant" because it is important for a servant to be reliable and dependable to receive a "well done"!

Thus, when it comes to selecting a successor, a successor needs to be both reliable and dependable! If a person cannot be dependable or reliable while you are alive, can you depend or rely upon them when you are dead? If one is consistently unreliable or undependable and has never demonstrated a good work ethic or spirit of excellence when it comes to ministry; then that person may not be a suitable successor. Someone who repeatedly misses service, meetings, deadlines; makes promises that they never keep; gives reactive excuses rather than proactive explanations; generating good ideas but lacks follow-through - is not prepared to be a leader or for that matter, in charge of anything.

Should tenure matter? Is there a requisite or minimum amount of time needed for a successor to prove that they are sufficiently reliable and dependable? When Paul gave instructions to Timothy regarding deacons, he said "and let these also first be proved; then let them use the office of a deacon, being found blameless" (I Timothy 3:10). How long does it take to be proven? Scripture gives us a vast range. Peter was only with Jesus for 3 years; whereas Joshua was with Moses for 40 years; and then somewhere in the middle we have the time Elisha spent with Elijah[25]. The answer may not be in the number of years, but in the number of assignments or the quantity of time spent together within a certain time frame.

---

[25] Bible scholars give Elisha tenure of service to Elijah somewhere between 6-12 years. Elijah accepted his call about four years before the death of Israel's King Ahab. For the next seven or eight years, Elisha became Elijah's close attendant until Elijah was taken up into heaven.

For example, a college course can be offered over a 16-week semester or in a 2-week intensive format. Both courses cover the same material, require the same tests and projects, and the same amount of total time in the classroom. However, semester courses have horizontal-time: short time, daily, over a series of weeks, whereas the intensive, vertical-time: long time, daily, over a few days. Another analogy would be that of test driving a car. One does not have to place thousands of miles on a car to test drive it. Often one can determine the quality of a vehicle as soon as it is driven off the parking lot. How the protégé responds to time-restraints, urgent deadlines, undesirable tasks, unglamorous assignments, emergency situations, disagreements, or sensitive matters can all aid in assessing whether the person is reliable and dependable.

You already know that some people have a horrible say-to-do ratio. These individuals always say, "Pastor, I got it!" but you find out later that they never got it done! Similarly, there are individuals who always have an excuse for not being available. The parable that Jesus gave in Luke 14:18-21 (NIV): ""But they all alike began to make excuses. The first said, 'I have just bought a field, and I must go and see it. Please excuse me.' "Another said, 'I have just bought five yokes of oxen, and I'm on my way to try them out. Please excuse me.' "Still another said, 'I just got married, so I can't come.' "The servant came back and reported this to his master. Then the owner of the house became angry and ordered his servant, 'Go out quickly into the streets and alleys of the town and bring in the poor, the crippled, the blind and the lame."

Too often, pastors have tried to give potential successors the opportunity to serve and even shine. However, too often the reply to the invitation is full of the same excuses over and over again. Eventually, the leader will lose confidence in an individual to be available or get the job done; and move on to someone else. Dear protégé, don't miss your chance to shoot your shot because you were unavailable to enter the game when the coach calls you!

Further, consideration should be made as to whether a preacher, that is only engaged when they have the microphone or the spotlight, is suitable to be a successor. Not only do you know the answer, but the people know it, too. It is no coincidence that the first verse of the Book of Joshua introduces Joshua as the son of Nun and "Moses's minister." When King Jehoshaphat was searching for a prophet from the Lord, an officer recommended Elisha, son of Shaphat, "who poured water on the hands of Elijah." In both instances, Joshua and Elisha's credibility was established based on who they had served. In life, opportunities will be afforded, credibility given, and doors opened, not because of your name, but because of your reputation for serving someone else. Who you serve, and how you serve, matters!

Granted, there may be a myriad of reasons why a person is inconsistent or irresponsible, and a person may mature over time or "step up" when it is their time to lead. Understandably, one might need grace when experiencing a difficult season in their lives. However, if after giving the individual multiple tasks or assignments, and they fail to show up, report, execute, or complete a task, on time, or to your standards; then that person may not be a suitable candidate to be a successor. Seasons do change, but an opportunity to serve may only come once in a lifetime. Ultimately, what made Joshua and Elisha suitable as successors to Moses and Elijah? It was their leader's ability to both, rely and depend on them, to get the job done, and get it done right!

CASE STUDY: NEW BIRTH MISSIONARY BAPTIST CHURCH

Following the passing of Bishop Eddie L. Long in 2017 and the resignation of his initial successor, Bishop Stephen A. Davis in 2018, New Birth Missionary Baptist Church in Atlanta was experiencing a significant decline in attendance and income. The church began a national search to find its next pastor. The selection committee included Bishop Long's widow, Elder Vanessa Long. The selection committee held several "listening

89

sessions" with the congregation to determine the characteristics of the individual who they desired to be selected as the next pastor[26]

Hundreds of names, including some of the most famous, well known, and respected; who's who list of preachers, applied and were interviewed for the job. Ultimately, New Birth selected Dr. Jamaal Harrison Bryant. Two factors weighed against him in the selection process: (1) his doctrine: Dr. Bryant was born and raised in the African Methodist Episcopal (AME) church, whereas New Birth was affiliated with the Missionary Baptist Church[27]; (2) character: Dr. Bryant was divorced from his wife and mother of his children after publicly known and acknowledged affair with another woman. However, weighing favorably for Dr. Bryant was his age, vision, leadership abilities, call to pastor, and even reliability and dependability. Also prior to founding the Empowerment Temple AME Church in Baltimore, MD, Dr. Bryant had served, for a brief time, at New Birth under the leadership of Bishop Long while in college at Morehouse College.

Only the passage of time can ultimately reveal whether Dr. Bryant was God's choice, but his immediate impact is undeniable. Under Dr. Bryant's leadership, New Birth has had a "rebirth", with thousands in attendance, live and virtually, each week; hundreds becoming members of

---

[26] New Birth's Bishop Stephen A. Davis comments on leaving DeKalb megachurch

https://www.ajc.com/lifestyles/new-birth-bishop-stephen-davis-resigns/Zq40FKMgJal0f9DkrexXfL/ published June 6, 2018, retrieved May 27, 2020.

[27] Some would argue that the distinction in doctrine between AME and Missionary Baptist is merely being two sides of the same coin. However, there are some fundamental differences in doctrine. Namely, when it comes to baptism (AME permits infant baptism, Missionary Baptist do not; AME permits sprinkling, but Missionary Baptist baptize by immersion, only) and form of church governance (AME has episcopal government with ownership and control over its churches whereas Missionary Baptist are autonomous churches with each church having a congregational form of government).

the church each Sunday; and initiating community outreach programs that have garnered national attention. It was also speculated in the media that he and his former wife were dating each other again. No doubt, New Birth is once again one of the leading churches, not only in Atlanta, but in America, because of its selection of Dr. Jamaal Bryant as successor to Bishop Eddie L. Long.

CALLING TO PASTOR

"And I will give you pastors according to mine heart, which shall feed you with knowledge and understanding" (Jeremiah 3:15 KJV). Jesus asked Peter three times if Peter loved him. In John 21:17 (KJV) says, "He saith unto him the third time, Simon, son of Jonas, lovest thou me? Peter was grieved because he said unto him the third time, Lovest thou me? And he said unto him, Lord, thou knowest all things; thou knowest that I love thee. Jesus saith unto him, Feed my sheep."

Peter in his epistles to the churches in Asia Minor, takes his charge from Jesus and passes it on to the next generation of pastors when he says,

"Feed the flock of God which is among you, taking the oversight thereof, not by constraint, but willingly; not for filthy lucre, but of a ready mind; Neither as being lords over God's heritage, but being examples to the flock. And when the chief Shepherd shall appear, ye shall receive a crown of glory that fadeth not away." I Peter 5:2-4 (KJV).

Other notable translations say it like this:

ASV   "according to the will of God; nor yet for filthy lucre, but of a ready mind"

GNB   "...as God wants you to, and not unwillingly. Do your work, not for mere pay, but from a real desire to serve"

ESV   "not under compulsion, but willingly, as God would have you; not for shameful gain, but eagerly"

ICB   "Watch over it because you want to, not because you are forced to do it. That is how God wants it. Do it because you are happy to serve, not because you want money."

From this we understand that an individual must have the: (1) call to pastor, (2) desire or willingness to pastor, and (3) right reasons for wanting to pastor. Even when providing the criteria for one to serve as a bishop, Paul first said, "if any many desire the office of a bishop." No true son or daughter will be eager to replace their mother or father in the gospel. Naturally, they may be apprehensive, reluctant, and even feel inadequate to do the job. But in the end, they must know that God has called them to the position. A person should not become a pastor because someone (other than God, of course) made them _do_ it; nor can it be because people expect them to _be_ it. If a person accepts the responsibility to pastor merely out of a sense of obligation and not from a sense of purpose, then they will either: not last long, be unsuccessful at it, or hate doing it.

Moreover, being a good preacher alone, does not guarantee that one will be a successful pastor. We have to take into account the 5-fold[28] ministry. It could very well be that an individual is called to preach but has a different capacity or role to play in ministry other than becoming a pastor. Ephesians 4:11-16 (KJV) reads, "And he gave some, apostles; and some, prophets; and some, evangelists; and some, pastors and teachers; For the perfecting of the saints, for the work of the ministry, for the edifying of the body of Christ:"

Paul instructs Timothy "But watch thou in all things, endure afflictions, do the work of an evangelist, make full proof of thy ministry"(II Timothy 4:5 KJV). The phrase "full proof" means to fulfill, carry out, to perform one's duty. In Colossians 4:17 (KJV) Paul instructs Archippus, "take heed to the ministry which thou hast received in the Lord, that thou fulfill it." One could infer that for Paul to make this special appeal to Archippus, that Archippus must have had a unique assignment, different from the others that Paul had saluted in his letter, and that unique assignment had to be completed by Archippus.

---

[28] Some scholars believe that the 5-fold ministry is only a 4-fold ministry. With the adjective "some" missing before the word 'teachers" they conclude that pastors and teachers are one in the same office.

Further we read in Paul's writings to Timothy and Titus, that Paul also makes distinctions between the offices of deacons, elders, and bishops (See I Timothy 3:1-3; Titus 1:5-9). Together, these Scriptures further support the notion that everyone is not made or called to serve alike in the church. "And God hath set some in the church, first apostles, secondarily prophets, thirdly teachers, after that miracles, then gifts of healings, helps, governments, diversities of tongues." (I Corinthians 12:28 KJV). Too many apostles, prophets and evangelists are operating outside of their office because they were taught that every preacher should aspire to pastor a church. Perhaps there would be fewer churches, and less frustrated preachers, if the church better recognized and appreciated, equally, the different roles and assignments of ministers in the Kingdom.

That being the case, how can one decipher between someone who is called to "preach" and someone who is called to "pastor"? There is not a set list of characteristics for being a pastor. However, there are some traits to consider: a servants heart, a soul-winner, cares for the people, attentive to the needs of others, proactive in ministering, desires to see people grow in God, able to teach and mentor others, and of their own volition, calls and prays (not preys) for people. Are they willing to do the extra things without recognition or compensation?

Noting Peter earlier, he further writes, "Whoever preaches must preach God's messages; whoever serves must serve with the strength that God gives, so that in all things praise may be given to God through Jesus Christ, to whom belong glory and power for ever and ever. Amen." (1 Peter 4:11 GNB)

It's hard for someone to pastor people and not like people! When pastoring, one is in the "business of people" and if a person is not a "people-person" or good with people, in general, then they will not likely succeed as a pastor. A shepherd has to be willing to spend countless hours in close proximity with the sheep. A hireling might be able to maintain the sheep, but a true shepherd will be able to care for the sheep. A true shepherd will not only get their hands dirty but have the smell of sheep on them. Which one of your sons or daughters in ministry has "dirt on their hands" and the "smell of sheep" on their clothes?

CONGREGATION'S PREFERENCE

Perhaps an individual has the call not just to preach but to also pastor a church. However, who do you think the congregation is willing to follow? Whether the successor was appointed or elected, if the congregation does not approve of who has been selected as a successor, it will quickly manifest with a precipitous decline in offerings or attendance. For many churches, gone are the days where a person is a member of a church from cradle to grave; regardless of who the pastor is of the church. For better or worse, people are more loyal or have allegiance to a particular pastor, preacher or personality, than to a particular church or congregation. One cannot force an unwanted or undesirable choice for a pastor, upon the people, and then expect them to stay and follow them. The Scripture records in I Kings 1:39 (KJV) upon the anointing of Solomon as king of Israel, that "all the people said, God save King Solomon. And all people piped with pipes, and rejoiced with great joy, so that the earth rent with the sound of them."

Similarly, in II Kings 2: 12 (KJV) after the mantle fell from Elijah to Elisha, it was his fellow prophets who declared, "The spirit of Elijah doth rest on Elisha." Moreover, the Scripture says, "and they came to meet him, and bowed themselves to the ground before him." After the death of Moses, the officers affirmed their support for Joshua. Deuteronomy 34:1(KJV) records, "And Joshua the son of Nun was full of the spirit of wisdom; for Moses had laid his hands upon him: and the children of Israel hearkened unto him, and did as the Lord commanded Moses." Joshua 1:16-17 (KJV) adds further, "And they answered Joshua, saying, all that thou commandest us we will do, and whithersoever thou sendest us, we will go. According as we hearkened unto Moses in all things, so will we hearken unto thee: only the LORD thy God be with thee, as he was with Moses."

94

Thus, who do you think the congregation will be willing to "obey," listen to, follow, and support; has to be taken into consideration. With an election, a congregation can express its preference by voting. However, if succession is done by appointment rather than by election, the leader must consider the congregation's preference. Under an appointment method, the congregation's preference is not an absolute or sole determinant but should not be completely dismissed either.

As stated in the opening of this book, a successor will either: buildup, maintain, or demolish the ministry. Who will your sons and daughters support? Who will the church officials and auxiliary leaders support? Will the church merely maintain its "money" and "membership", or will there be an immediate or sharp decline in income or attendance under the next leader? Will the people "rejoice" or "weep" at the consecration of the successor you selected to be the next pastor? Dear pastor, whatever you do, don't ignore the people's preference in the selection process!

GOD'S CHOICE

Setting aside one's own personal preferences, candidate resumes, and the people's choice; ultimately, it should be God's decision as to who will lead his people next. In the end, HE is the owner and boss of the church, and pastors are merely its managers and employees. We might be able to train or recommend someone for the job, but in the end, it is God's decision to hire or promote someone. We can't ignore that God decided that Joshua would succeed Moses, Solomon would succeed David, and Elisha would succeed Elijah. Even Samuel placed emphasis on the wrong criteria when seeking a son of Jesse to replace Saul as king of Israel. Nor can we overlook the fact that God told Eli, Samuel, and Saul, that their sons would not succeed them in leadership. However, God did show Eli, Samuel; Samuel, Saul; and Saul, David. Eli, Samuel or Saul may not have liked God's decision, but they had to accept it! The level of achievement accomplished by their successors, speak for themselves, and that God's choice was the right choice! A leader should not settle for a "good" decision when a church needs a "God" decision. A congregation deserves not just the "best" choice for pastor, but the "blessed" choice for pastor!

QUESTIONS FOR REFLECTION
1. Which characteristic is the most important to you and why?
2. Which characteristic is the least important to you and why?
3. How would your rank the characteristic from 1-10, with 1 being the most important and 10 being the least important?
4. How do you think your list would compare to another pastor or the members in your congregation? What would be the reason for your difference in opinion?
5. Which characteristic would you remove from the list? Any characteristic you would add to the list? Why?

CHAPTER 7
THE IMPORTANCE OF MENTORSHIP: DO YOU HAVE RUTH OR TIMOTHY?

"MENTORS TURN THEIR LOSSES INTO YOUR LESSONS. WHOSE VOICE ARE YOU ALLOWING TO GIVE YOU GUIDANCE IN THIS SEASON?"
~ ELDER MARK MOORE, JR.

The relationships of Naomi and Ruth and Paul and Timothy are different from the other relationships noted in this book. Ruth and Timothy did not necessarily inherit a kingdom, ministry, or mantle from their mentors. However, Ruth and Timothy did receive an impartation of wisdom, encouragement, and prayer from their mentors that enabled them to succeed in life and ministry. The impartation from mentor to mentee, ultimately became a boomerang blessing back on the mentor from the mentee.

Paul writes to the church at Corinth, "For though ye have ten thousand instructors in Christ yet *have ye* not many fathers: for in Christ Jesus I have begotten you through the gospel." (I Corinthians 4:15 KJV). It's been said, instructors tell you the way, but mentors and fathers show you the way. Or in other words, one can either teach you how to do it (instructors) or show you how it has been done (fathers and mentors). Understand, neither Naomi and Ruth nor Paul and Timothy were biologically related to each other, yet their relationships could be described as mother-daughter and father-son, respectfully.

Moreover, in the context of succession planning, Ruth and Timothy represent sons and daughters that have a different assignment from their mentors. However, the relationship and impact on each is in no ways diminished. Understand that a Ruth or Timothy might not be in your direct

97

line of succession, but you have been assigned to ensure that they succeed in their God-given assignment.

NAOMI AND RUTH

The Book of Ruth begins with a story about a grieving and despondent woman by the name of Naomi. Naomi is preparing to return to her hometown to live the rest of her life alone, impoverished, and dependent on the generosity of her family for her survival. With no money and having lost her husband and two sons, Naomi was returning home believing that her best days were behind her. With nothing else to live for, Naomi had resigned herself to spend the remaining days of her life as a broken and sorrowful woman.

I.   Mentors Live A Life Worth Following

Initially, Naomi was to be accompanied by both of her daughters-in-law, Ruth and Orpah. Heeding the advice of Naomi, Orpah decided to remain in Moab. However, Ruth chose to affirm her allegiance to Naomi and returned with Naomi back to Judah. One cannot forget Ruth's pledge to Naomi, "*The women cried together again. Then Orpah kissed Naomi good-bye, but Ruth held on to her. Naomi said, "Look, your sister-in-law is going back to her own people and her own gods. Go back with her." But Ruth said, "Don't ask me to leave you! Don't beg me not to follow you! Every place you go, I will go. Every place you live, I will live. Your people will be my people. Your God will be my God. And where you die, I will die. And there I will be buried. I ask the Lord to punish me terribly if I do not keep this promise: Only death will separate us." Naomi saw that Ruth had made up her mind to go with her. So, Naomi stopped arguing with her. (Ruth 1:14-18 ICB)*

II.   Mentees are Willing to Submit to Mentor's Instructions

Upon returning to Bethlehem, Naomi instructs Ruth on not just how to survive as a widow but how to secure a new husband and establish long-term financial security. Naomi's instructions ultimately led Ruth to find her destiny. Naomi informs Ruth about their wealthy kinsman by the name of

Boaz. Upon Ruth's suggestion, Naomi gives Ruth permission to glean in Boaz's field. It is there that Boaz sees Ruth, learns of her story and extends an invitation for her to glean in his field.

Boaz gives Ruth special privileges to glean in his fields without restrictions or limitations. He tells his servants to leave behind extra for Ruth to glean. Upon learning of Ruth's encounter with Boaz, Naomi instructs Ruth to (1) work near Boaz's maidens; (2) avoid visiting other fields to glean; (3) continue this routine until the end of the barley and wheat harvest; and (4) remain with her throughout the process (Ruth 2:1-23). In other words, Naomi taught Ruth that in order to be promoted one must be loyal, consistent, visibly productive, and maintain good character. Without heeding to Naomi's wise counsel, Ruth may have been viewed as a mere opportunist seeking selfish gain.

Naomi also taught Ruth the importance of timing and how to navigate a unique opportunity. Waiting until the end of the harvest, Naomi instructs Ruth how to approach Boaz. Understanding that Boaz has had an entire season to observe, and possibly become attracted to Ruth, Naomi gives Ruth specific instructions before attending Boaz's end of the harvest party. Naomi further instructs Ruth to wait until after Boaz had a few drinks and had fallen asleep to "uncover his feet" and lay down. The Scriptures state that Boaz got drunk, crashed on a heap of corn, and woke up at midnight with a woman laying at his feet.

For the sake of argument, if one literally interprets "uncovering feet" to mean that nothing sexual happened between Ruth and Boaz, Ruth's presence at Boaz's awakening had to get his attention. Moreover, this was probably the first time Boaz saw Ruth "fix herself up" in anything more than dirty work clothes. Boaz immediately set out to make Ruth his wife. Being the end of the harvest, Boaz had the money and the time to marry and care for a new wife. Naomi's plan worked perfectly! Naomi was a great coach, but equally important, Ruth was a great student. Naomi successfully mentored Ruth to the point of not just surviving in her new environment but positioned Ruth to flourish in it.

III.   Mentor's Rejoice at Mentee's Accomplishments

Through a series of events, Boaz would eventually marry Ruth and she would bear a son, Obed. When news reached Naomi that Ruth had given birth, the women in the town declared to Naomi that Ruth's son, "... shall be unto thee a restorer of thy life, and a nourisher of thine old age; for thy daughter in law, which loveth thee, which is better to thee than seven sons, hath born him" Ruth 4:15 (KJV).

Naomi, so excited about the news of her mentee, Ruth, giving birth to a son by Boaz; the bible says that that it stimulated Naomi's dried breast to nurse again. Biologically, Ruth's son was not even related to Naomi! However, for Naomi to be so excited about the success of Ruth to the point that it restored the milk in Naomi's breast; is nothing short of a miracle! Yes, it may be feasible for a woman to nurse another woman's child, referred to as wet nursing. However, wet nursing is conditioned upon the woman having maintained her ability to nurse after giving birth to her own children. Is it reasonable to conclude that if Naomi's two sons were old enough to marry that Naomi had not nursed a baby in several decades?

Thus, it was only the sure love, joy, excitement, and hand of God that would allow Naomi's breast to help feed and nourish Ruth's newborn baby. As a mentor, can you get so excited about the success of your mentee that it restores life in you again? Will you experience Naomi's level of excitement when you see your mentee's ministry succeed, perhaps outgrow yours, walk on bigger platforms, or meet people on a different level of ministry? Naomi did not get jealous or envious of her daughter in law's success, for she was still a widow without any living biological children, yet she rejoiced as if Ruth's child was biologically her own.

IV.   Mentees Share Their Success with Their Mentors

Equally important, a mentee should never forget, ignore, or think they are better than their mentor. Ruth could have easily moved on her with life, new husband, new baby, new status, and new wealth. However, Ruth did not forget or ignore Naomi, but allowed her to help nurse her baby and even claim it as a "son born to Naomi."

Ruth understood that it took Naomi to put her in a position to give birth to Obed, but also understood that she would need Naomi to help raise Obed. You will need Naomi to help you get to where you are going, but you will also need Naomi to help you stay there once you arrive! One never outgrows individuals like Naomi. Whereas instructors may be for a season, mothers and mentors are for life!

Thus, in order to have a Naomi-Ruth relationship, Naomi must be secure enough to celebrate, and not envy the success of Ruth, while Ruth must be humble enough to remember, and not forget that her success came because of Naomi. How beautiful, beneficial, and mutually gratifying to have sacrificed one's self for the benefit of another, to then have that person feed you fruit from the tree that you helped them to plant. Even in their mutual celebration of the birth of Obed, neither of them could have foreseen David or Jesus down the genealogical line. Know that the fruit of your mentorship relationship may not only be enjoyed in your lifetime but be a blessing to the world for eternity!

PAUL AND TIMOTHY

In the book of Acts, we first meet Timothy in Chapter 16, during what is known as Paul's second missionary journey. On the first journey, Paul had founded churches in the southern part of what we call Asia Minor or Turkey, at Iconium, Lystra, and Derbe. Revisiting these churches on his second journey (Acts 15:36-41), he apparently met Timothy for the first time in Lystra. Paul picks the young disciple to accompany, assist, and serve as a sort of apprentice under him. Timothy's biological father was Greek, but no evidence is ever given that he was a Christian. So, Paul filled the shoes of a spiritual father to Timothy."

Paul affirms Timothy's call and gifting in ministry twice: first by the laying on of hands by the presbytery and second by Paul's own hands himself (I Timothy 4:14; II Timothy 1:6). Paul would later recommend him to the church at Philippians (Philippians 2:19-23). In six of Paul's letters he makes reference to Timothy as a brother or servant in sending his letter to the church (See II Corinthians 1:1; Philippians 1:1; Colossians 1:1; I & II Thessalonians 1:1, and Philemon 1:1). In Romans, Paul refers to Timothy as a fellow worker. (Romans 16:21). As recorded in Acts chapters 16-20, Timothy traveled extensively for Paul, in his stead, visiting churches Paul had established and reported their condition back to him.

"We sent Timothy, who is our brother and co-worker in God's service in spreading the gospel of Christ, to strengthen and encourage you in your faith... But Timothy has just now come to us from you and has brought good news about your faith and love. He has told us that you always have pleasant memories of us and that you long to see us, just as we also long to see you." (I Thessalonians 3:2, 6 NIV).

The Bible informs us that Paul ultimately assigned Timothy to lead the church in Ephesus becoming its first bishop and overseer (I Timothy 1:3). Church history tells us that Timothy was ultimately killed as a martyr[29].

I.   Mentors Endorse and Promote Mentees

As noted, in Paul's letter to Philippians and four times in his epistle to Timothy, Paul refers to Timothy as his son[30]: I Timothy 1: 2 "Unto Timothy, my own son in the faith" I Timothy 1:18 "This charge I commit unto thee, son Timothy" II Timothy 1:2 "to Timothy, my dearly beloved son" II Timothy 2:1 "my son, be strong in the grace." Similar to Ruth, Timothy's reputation preceded him because of his service to his mentor. Paul writes

---

[29] "Although not stated in the bible, other sources have records of the apostle's death. The apocryphal Acts of Timothy states that in the year 97 AD, the 80-year-old bishop tried to halt a procession in honor of the goddess Diana by preaching the gospel. The angry pagans beat him, dragged him through the streets, and stoned him to death."
https://en.wikipedia.org/wiki/Saint_Timothy#cite_note-oca-10

[30] Paul also uses the word "son" in his writing to Titus and in his writing to Philemon about Onesimus. However, with Timothy, Paul refers to Timothy as son repeatedly, both publicly and privately, and in more than one of his letters.

in Philippians "But ye know the proof of him, that, as a son with the father, he hath served with me in the gospel."

In other words, Paul is saying, "if you trust me, you can trust him", because he has served faithfully beside me in doing the work of the ministry. A note to sons: can your spiritual father say that about you to others? Can your pastor say to another pastor, "I can't make this speaking engagement, but am sending my associate minister, and he is just as good as having me with you"? In Philippians 2:19-23, Paul writes,

"I hope in the Lord Jesus to send Timothy to you soon, that I also may be cheered when I receive news about you. I have no one else like him, who will show genuine concern for your welfare. For everyone looks out for their own interests, not those of Jesus Christ. But you know that Timothy has proved himself, because as a son with his father he has served with me in the work of the gospel. I hope, therefore, to send him as soon as I see how things go with me."

II.   Mentors Instruct and Inspire Mentees

Moreover, what is significant about Paul's relationship with Timothy is that we have two epistles, personal letters, written from father to son. In using these letters for doctrine, we often forget their original audience and purpose as personal letters. Just think how these words, written to someone else centuries ago, bless us today; how much more they must have blessed Timothy during his life and ministry.

Paul gives Timothy instruction on church governance, lessons about false doctrine, teaching on domestic life, caution against the potential pitfalls of not only what to avoid, but who to avoid! Further, Paul also gives Timothy endearing words of encouragement "fight the good fight of faith," "let no man despise thy youth," "neglect not the gift that is within thee," and to "keep that which is committed to thy trust," and to "study to show thyself approved." Finally, Paul in what is considered to be his last letter written to anyone, informs Timothy of what to expect in the last days, gives his final farewell, and provides Timothy with his famous final charge:

"I charge thee therefore before God, and the Lord Jesus Christ, who shall judge the quick and the dead at his appearing and his kingdom; Preach the word; be instant in season, out of season; reprove, rebuke, exhort with all long suffering and doctrine. For the time will come when they will not endure sound doctrine; but after their own lusts shall they heap to themselves teachers, having itching ears; And they shall turn away their ears from the truth, and shall be turned unto fables. But watch thou in all things, endure afflictions, do the work of an evangelist, make full proof of thy ministry." (II Timothy 4:1-4 KJV)

Imagine if more founders, mentors, apostolic fathers took the time to put in letters or books: advice and admonition, best practices, do's and don'ts, FAQ, of life and ministry for the future generation to retain and read. This is why presidents have libraries archiving their personal papers and even letters. They reveal something about the person that we might not see in the public persona. While saying it is good, memories fade and things are forgotten, but to take the time to write or record a personal letter to a mentee, something that can be reread or replayed over and over again, giving advice, encouragement, and instruction, especially in times of need, can be a tremendous source of strength that will ensure the success of the mentee.

IV. A Mentor Can Cut You Where It Hurts

Finally, Timothy is special as a son not just because Paul took favor with him and brought him under his wing, nor solely because Timothy was a faithful and reliable assistant. Acts 16:1-5, states that Timothy allowed Paul to circumcise him, "Paul wanted Timothy to travel with him. But all the Jews living in that area knew that Timothy's father was Greek. So, Paul circumcised Timothy to please the Jews." (Acts 16:3 ICB)

Remember, while Timothy was young, he was not a child or infant, but a grown man or at least an adolescent teenager. Thus, to allow another man to have access to your most vulnerable, sensitive, intimate area of your body to cut away excess foreskin so that you can be acceptable to others

104

for ministry requires a level of trust, commitment, and sacrifice on a completely different level.

Please do not misconstrue or pervert this in any way, but the question must be asked: can your father in the gospel circumcise you? There are numerous biblical examples of fathers circumcising their own sons. Can your father in the gospel rebuke, reprimand, refine, chisel you in your most private areas of life, to make you more acceptable in ministry; and you still serve them faithfully until the very end? An instructor might be able to correct a student, but a father must be able to circumcise his son. For more study on the relationship between Paul and Timothy, considering reading articles by Stacy E. Hoehl[31], Rick Warren[32], and Christianity Today[33].

In closing, there are six principles about mentorship that can be derived from the relationship of Naomi and Ruth and Paul and Timothy. First, mentors live a life worth submitting to and following. Second, mentors rejoice and take pride at the success and accomplishments of their mentees. Thirdly, mentors will help your raise and nurse your "new baby". Fourthly, mentors will use their name and reputation to help promote and endorse their mentees to others. Fifthly, mentors provide both instruction and inspiration. They remind you of who you are and what you are destined to become in life. Lastly, a mentor can be trusted enough to cut the

---

[31] "THE MENTOR RELATIONSHIP: AN EXPLORATION OF PAUL AS LOVING MENTOR TO TIMOTHY AND THE APPLICATION OF THIS RELATIONSHIP TO CONTEMPORARY LEADERSHIP CHALLENGES" Journal of Biblical Perspectives in Leadership 3, no. 2 (Summer 2011), 32-47. © 2011 School of Global Leadership & Entrepreneurship, Regent University ISSN 1941-4692, https://www.regent.edu/acad/global/publications/jbpl/vol3no2/JBPL_Vol3No2_Hoehl_pp32-47.pdf

[32] 3 Phases of a Paul and Timothy Relationship, February 6, 2014, https://pastors.com/paul-timothy/

[33] Who Was Timothy in the Bible? How Did He Help Paul? Originally published June 10, 2012 by Christianity Today. https://www.christianity.com/bible/people-of-the-bible/st-timothy-pauls-associate-11629587.html

mentee's most intimate and private areas of life to prepare them for the next dimension of ministry.

QUESTIONS FOR REFLECTION
1. Why do you think Ruth was willing to follow Naomi and submit to her instructions?
2. Why is it sometimes hard for mentors to celebrate the success of mentees?
3. How important is it for mentees to share their successes with their mentors?
4. If you were Paul writing a letter to Timothy, what would you tell him?
5. Why is it hard for mentees to accept rebuke, correction, or "cutting" from their mentor? Is it because most mentors have not earned the trust and respect of their mentee or is it because most mentees are not willing to submit or participate in a cutting or refining process by their mentors?

CHAPTER 8
ISN'T THE CHURCH A FAMILY BUSINESS?
NEPOTISM IN SUCCESSION PLANNING

"NEPOTISM SOMETIMES CAN BE A LOSE-LOSE SITUATION."
~ VIKRAM CHATWAL

Nepotism simply defined is favoritism shown to relatives, especially in appointment to desirable positions. It may be the desire of the pastor or most prominent family in the church for a son, a daughter, or someone closely related to them to become the next leader. However, this is not always God's plan! Unlike a family business that belongs to the owner and its shareholders, the church is owned by God and it is ultimately up to God to decide who He wants to lead His people next. In many cases, God does honor the leader by granting their desire for an heir or family member, (in some cases multiple family members over several generations) to lead a particular congregation.

For example, God promises David through the prophet Nathan, "And it shall come to pass, when thy days be expired that thou must go to be with thy fathers, that I will raise up thy seed after thee, which shall be of thy sons; and I will establish his kingdom. He shall build me an house, and I will stablish his throne forever. I will be his father, and he shall be my son: and I will not take my mercy away from him, as I took it from him that was before thee: But I will settle him in mine house and in my kingdom forever: and his throne shall be established for evermore. According to all these words, and according to all this vision, so did Nathan speak unto David." (I Chronicles 17:11-15 KJV).

Likewise, God gives Phinehas a similar promise as it relates to descendants and the office of the priesthood. "Phinehas, the son of Eleazar, the son of Aaron the priest, hath turned my wrath away from the children of Israel, while he was zealous for my sake among them, that I consumed not the children of Israel in my jealousy. Wherefore say, Behold, I give unto him my covenant of peace: And he shall have it, and his seed after him, even the covenant of an everlasting priesthood; because he was zealous for his God, and made an atonement for the children of Israel" (Numbers 25:10-13 KJV).

However, to automatically assume this will happen or to force it to happen, when God has not clearly sanctioned, or even is expressly opposed to it, can be a sure recipe for disaster in the future for a church. For various reasons, God may reject a son and select someone from a different gender, generation, or family. A careful examination of the following leaders will illustrate how there may be a variety of reasons why God does not select an heir-apparent to be the successor. However, in each case, when God did appoint someone else to be the successor, God ensured that the successor had a prosperous life, ministry, or administration.

MOSES AND HIS SONS: GERSHOM AND ELIEZER

"And thou shalt take this rod in thine hand, wherewith thou shalt do signs. And Moses went and returned to Jethro his father in law, and said unto him, let me go, I pray thee, and return unto my brethren which are in Egypt, and see whether they be yet alive. And Jethro said to Moses, Go in peace. And the LORD said unto Moses in Midian, Go, return into Egypt: for all the men are dead which sought thy life. And Moses took his wife and his sons, and set them upon an ass, and he returned to the land of Egypt: and Moses took the rod of God in his hand.

And it came to pass by the way in the inn, that the LORD met him, and sought to kill him. Then Zipporah took a sharp stone, and cut off the foreskin of her son, and cast it at his feet, and said, Surely a bloody husband

108

art thou to me. So, he let him go: then she said, A bloody husband thou art, because of the circumcision" (Exodus 4: 17-20, 24-26 KJV).[34]

"When Jethro, the priest of Midian, Moses' father in law, heard of all that God had done for Moses, and for Israel his people, and that the LORD had brought Israel out of Egypt; Then Jethro, Moses' father in law, took Zipporah, Moses' wife, after he had sent her back, And her two sons; of which the name of the one was Gershom; for he said, I have been an alien in a strange land: And the name of the other was Eliezer; for the God of my father, said he, was mine help, and delivered me from the sword of Pharaoh: And Jethro, Moses' father in law, came with his sons and his wife unto Moses into the wilderness, where he encamped at the mount of God: And he said unto Moses, I thy father in law Jethro am come unto thee, and thy wife, and her two sons with her. And Moses went out to meet his father in law, and did obeisance, and kissed him; and they asked each other of their welfare; and they came into the tent" (Exodus 18:1-7, KJV).

The question must be asked: did Moses' decision to leave Midian to go to Egypt cause an irreparable breach in his marriage and family? As Moses, along with his wife and sons, are on their way to Egypt a death angel attacks Moses. After a series of events Zipporah discerns that the only way to prevent death from taking place was to circumcise her son (which should have been done by Moses years prior). After flinging the bloody foreskin cut from her son's body, it appears that Zipporah got scared and took her sons with her and went back to Midian. Not until after the 10 plagues and exodus, did Jethro bring Zipporah and sons to visit Moses in the wilderness.

Even when Jethro talks to Moses, there is no indication that his wife, nor his sons, were there to listen as Moses shared his testimony of

---

[34] For more discussion on this passage of Scripture, I encourage you to read Chapter 8 of *Crushing* © 2019 by Bishop T.D. Jakes. I also encourage you to read "Zipporah at the inn" https://en.wikipedia.org/wiki/Zipporah_at_the_inn retrieved August 15, 2020 and bible commentaries on Exodus 4:24 https://biblehub.com/commentaries/exodus/4-24.htm retrieved August 15, 2020.

what God had done to the Egyptians. Not to read too deep into it. Either Moses' sons were resentful of their father's ministry and its impact on their life or they simply had no interest in the father's ministry. Further, Moses wrote the Pentateuch but had very little to say about his own wife and children may also support the opinion that there was a breach in the family. When Jethro brings Moses' family to see him, they are presented as "thy wife and her two sons with her."

Moreover, Moses was criticized by Aaron and Miriam because "he had married an Ethiopian woman" (Numbers 121-12 KJV). Was Zipporah dead? Did Moses divorce Zipporah? Did Moses simply take on a second wife? Perhaps Aaron and Miriam were not critical of who Moses married but the fact that he got married. If we accept the chronology of the Book of Exodus and the Book of Numbers, then Moses is criticized for his Ethiopian wife prior to the incident with the 12-spies entering Canaan (Numbers 14:1-10).Therefore, Moses married the Ethiopian woman prior to the commencement of the 40 year "wandering in the wilderness" punishment (Numbers 14:34 KJV). Thereby suggesting that all of the aforementioned events with Moses and his family occurred within the first year after the exodus from Egypt.

According to the Book of Numbers[35] and the Book of I Chronicles[36]Moses' sons were simply integrated into the Levite tribe without

---

[35] **Numbers 3:1-4,** "These also are the generations of Aaron and Moses in the day that the LORD spake with Moses in mount Sinai. And these are the names of the sons of Aaron; Nadab the firstborn, and Abihu, Eleazar, and Ithamar. These are the names of the sons of Aaron, the priests which were anointed, whom he consecrated to minister in the priest's office. And Nadab and Abihu died before the LORD, when they offered strange fire before the LORD, in the wilderness of Sinai, and they had no children: and Eleazar and Ithamar ministered in the priest's office in the sight of Aaron their father."

[36] I Chronicles 23:1-17, "Now concerning Moses the man of God, his sons were named of the tribe of Levi. The sons of Moses were, Gershom, and Eleazar. Of the sons of Gershom, Shebuel was the chief. And the sons of Eleazar were,

any special privileges, responsibilities or status other than that which was afforded to all Levites. Various Hebrew traditions have emerged over time to explain what happened to Moses' sons. In essence, most arrive at the same conclusion that Moses' sons did not become anything special but became a regular part of the congregation.

What is the principle for succession planning learned from Moses and his sons? Parents cannot force their children to become the successor if after 40 years of service to a ministry or organization they have not demonstrated any discernible interest or commitment to it. God would in fact select Moses' nephews to become the priest. However, nothing is ever mentioned or suggested that Moses' sons had an active role at any point during the ministry or administration of Moses. It could have been that Gershom and Eliezer were resentful over how they lost their father and way of life in Midian after 40 years because of Moses' call to serve Israel. It also might have simply been that Gershom and Eliezer had their own lives and aspirations which did not include serving with their father in the wilderness.

Did Moses get so caught up in being a leader that he forgot how to be a father? When Jethro suggested that Moses was overworked from judging the people and recommended that Moses delegate, was it simply a matter of becoming a better administrator or a matter of creating more time to spend with his family? Jethro may have said, "Moses, your wife and kids are here to see you, but you are out here judging the people all day!" Whatever the case, it is apparent that Gershom and Eliezer saw what Moses did as "his" thing and not "our" thing. Thus, forcing a child into a position of leadership, when they have not served or demonstrated any discernible interest in the ministry, is unwise and fool hearted. In such cases, the best advice maybe to treat them as Moses did his sons - just let them be a member of the congregation!!

Rehabiah the chief. And Eleazar had none other sons; but the sons of Rehabiah were very many."

ZELOPHEHAD'S FIVE DAUGHTERS

"The daughters of Zelophehad son of Hepher, the son of Gilead, the son of Makir, the son of Manasseh, belonged to the clans of Manasseh son of Joseph. The names of the daughters were Mahlah, Noah, Hoglah, Milkah and Tirzah. They came forward and stood before Moses, Eleazar the priest, the leaders and the whole assembly at the entrance to the tent of meeting and said, "Our father died in the wilderness. He was not among Korah's followers, who banded together against the LORD, but he died for his own sin and left no sons. Why should our father's name disappear from his clan because he had no son? Give us property among our father's relatives."

So, Moses brought their case before the LORD, and the LORD said to him, "What Zelophehad's daughters are saying is right. You must certainly give them property as an inheritance among their father's relatives and give their father's inheritance to them.

"Say to the Israelites, 'If a man dies and leaves no son, give his inheritance to his daughter. If he has no daughter, give his inheritance to his brothers. If he has no brothers, give his inheritance to his father's brothers.[1] If his father had no brothers, give his inheritance to the nearest relative in his clan, that he may possess it. This is to have the force of law for the Israelites, as the LORD commanded Moses.'" (Numbers 27:1-3, 5-11, NIV – emphasis added)

This book is not intended to create a theological or doctrinal debate about the role of women in ministry. However, what if God does want to have one of your children to continue the work of the ministry; should it be viewed as impossible or improbable because there are no sons in the family? What if you are like Phillip, the father of 4 daughters, that all prophesy, then what do you do? What do you do if you have a Deborah in your midst that is anointed not only to prophecy but to judge the people, too? You may have daughters that bear all the characteristics of a good successor except for the fact that they are female rather than males. (See

Chapter 6 - Additional Characteristics of a Successor). Should natural or spiritual daughters in ministry be automatically disqualified or excluded from being mentored, trained as a protégé, or in the line of succession simply because of their gender?

Perhaps you may have a combination of sons and daughters, but your sons are not following in your footsteps, but your daughters walk in them daily. Should sons be pushed into ministry at the expense of daughters being pushed out of ministry? Like Moses you might have to "bring their case before the LORD," be open to whatever God has to say about it, and ultimately do, whatever he instructs you. Who knows God might use you and your daughters to set a new precedent for the people!

ELI AND HIS SONS: HOPHNI AND PHINEHAS

"Now the sons of Eli were sons of Belial; they knew not the LORD. And the priest's custom with the people was, that, when any man offered sacrifice, the priest's servant came, while the flesh was in seething, with a flesh hook of three teeth in his hand; And he struck it into the pan, or kettle, or caldron, or pot; all that the flesh hook brought up the priest took for himself. So, they did in Shiloh unto all the Israelites that came thither. Also, before they burnt the fat, the priest's servant came, and said to the man that sacrificed, give flesh to roast for the priest; for he will not have sodden flesh of thee, but raw. And if any man said unto him, Let them not fail to burn the fat presently, and then take as much as thy soul desireth; then he would answer him, Nay; but thou shalt give it me now: and if not, I will take it by force. Wherefore the sin of the young men was very great before the LORD: for men abhorred the offering of the LORD"

"And there came a man of God unto Eli, and said unto him, thus saith the LORD, Did I plainly appear unto the house of thy father, when they were in Egypt in Pharaoh's house? And did I choose him out of all the tribes of Israel to be my priest, to offer upon mine altar, to burn incense, to wear an ephod before me? and did I give unto the house of thy father all the offerings made by fire of the children of Israel? Wherefore kick ye at my sacrifice and at mine offering, which I have commanded in my habitation; and honourest thy sons above me, to make yourselves fat with the chiefest of all the offerings of Israel my people?"

"And this shall be a sign unto thee, that shall come upon thy two sons, on Hophni and Phinehas; in one day they shall die both of them. And I will raise me up a faithful priest, that shall do according to that which is in mine heart and in my mind: and I will build him a sure house; and he shall walk before mine anointed forever." (I Samuel 2:12-17, 27-29, 34-35 KJV}

These passages share the judgment of God against the house of Eli and his two sons, Hophni and Phinehas. The Scriptures describe Hophni and Phinehas as sons of Belial or in other words: scoundrels, worthless men, wicked men, corrupt, base men, good-for-nothing priests, evil sons, sons of worthlessness. While entitled to a portion of the sacrifices, Hophni and Phinehas would take a disproportionate share of the sacrifices than what they were entitled. They would treat the worshipers with contempt and disrespect. They were also known to have had illicit and adulterous sex with the women who worshipped or served at the house of God.

These reprehensible behaviors mimicked the wicked behaviors of priests serving false and idolatrous gods. Hophni and Phinehas not only took advantage of the people, abused their privilege and authority, but also, consequently, turned the people away from serving and sacrificing to the true God in the house of God. In other words, the ones that should have been pointing people to God were in fact contributing to the people turning away from God! God forbid if we allow our churches to operate like the house of Eli - God will hold all of us accountable!

Some may argue, "Well, boys will be boys." However true or untrue that might be, God not only judged Hophni and Phinehas, but their father Eli for turning a blind eye and failing to correct his sons. Nowhere in Scripture does it record that Eli repented or tried to correct his sons after he had been warned. Remarkable, Eli's response was, "It is the Lord: let him do what seemeth him good." In other words, "it is what it is, and I can't do anything about it."

Without remorse, contrition, or repentance, Eli still did nothing! He could have at least told his sons what had been prophesied. Perhaps if Hophni and Phinehas knew their pending judgment , it could have provoked them to repent, and for God to have mercy on them. Consequently, Hophni and Phinehas would die by the hand of the Philistines. Upon hearing about his son's death and the capture of the ark of God, Eli fell over and died. Not only that, Phinehas pregnant wife died in labor. Her final words being the name she gave to her newborn son, "Ichabod" - for the glory has departed from Israel!

Eli's legacy was cut off, not just because his sons were corrupt, but because he failed to correct his sons when they were in error. God could have raised up Eli's grandson, Ichabod, to carry on the family ministry. However, as God declared, he would cut off his house and rise up someone else to be a faithful priest in their stead. No matter how much a leader may want to have their children to carry on the legacy, if they lack character and integrity, it is a disqualification for them to serve as a successor. What could have been, ended up not being, because of Eli and his sons, Hophni and Phinehas. Indeed, God will have to rise up a faithful priest to serve in their stead!

SAMUEL AND HIS SONS: JOEL AND ABIJAH

"When Samuel grew old, he appointed his sons as Israel's leaders. The name of his firstborn was Joel and the name of his second was Abijah, and they served at Beersheba. But his sons did not follow his ways. They turned aside after dishonest gain and accepted bribes and perverted justice. So, all the elders of Israel gathered together and came to Samuel at Ramah. They said to him, "You are old, and your sons do not follow your ways; now appoint a king to lead us, such as all the other nations have." But when they said, "Give us a king to lead us," this displeased Samuel; so, he prayed to the LORD. And the LORD told him:

115

"Listen to all that the people are saying to you; it is not you they have rejected, but they have rejected me as their king." (I Samuel 8:1-9, NIV)

Similar to Eli, Samuel appointed corrupt sons to positions of authority. Setting aside for a moment the matter of Israel demanding a king and Samuel feeling rejected as a judge; nothing in the text suggests that what the people said about Samuel's sons was incorrect. The Scripture gives credence to Samuel's character as a prophet, man of integrity, and one whose "words never fell to the ground". When Samuel died, the entire nation gathered to mourn for him.

Granted, in the big scheme of things, God had other plans, but if for the sake of argument, the Scripture is taken at face value, the people rejected Samuel's sons as his successor because of their lack of character and integrity. The people's indictment against Samuel's sons was not based on a personality conflict. The people did not reject Samuel's sons because they were displeased with their leadership style or jurisprudence. The people rejected Samuel's sons because they engaged in "dishonest gain and accepted bribes and perverted justice."

A question must be asked: did Samuel, as prophet, not know what his sons were doing behind his back? Was it possible for Samuel to expose the mess in Eli's house, but not see the mess in his own house? Yes, unfortunately, it is very well possible! Sometimes prophets can be blinded by love and overlook the sins of their own children. However, the more likely case is that Samuel knew, but ignored it for the sake of establishing a family legacy. If the latter is true, then Samuel became complicit in his son's immoral behavior. It's time for leaders to stop promoting their sons and daughters (biological and spiritual) to key positions based on nepotism; knowing that their children have a reputation for being unethical and unholy with the people. You might appoint them to lead, but ultimately the people will not follow corrupt leaders.

ZECHARIAH, THE SON OF BERECHIAH, THE SON OF IDDO THE PROPHET

"In the eighth month, in the second year of Darius, came the word of the LORD unto Zechariah, the son of Berechiah, the son of Iddo the prophet, saying,

Upon the four and twentieth day of the eleventh month, which is the month Sebat, in the second year of Darius, came the word of the LORD unto Zechariah, the son of Berechiah, the son of Iddo the prophet, saying," (Zechariah 1:1, 7 KJV)

Zechariah was a minor prophet also believed to be a part of the priest family concerned with the rebuilding of Jerusalem post exile. The Scripture notes that his grandfather was a prophet. Although little is known about Iddo, he appears in II Chronicles 13:22 "The other events of Abijah's reign...are written in the annotations of the prophet Iddo." Again, in II Chronicles 12:15 "As for the events of Rehoboam's reign...are they not written in the records of...Iddo the seer that deal with genealogies."

Berechiah, Zechariah's father is noted for working in the Temple, but not necessarily as a prophet, but more as priest. However, Zechariah took on more of the ministry of his grandfather, Iddo, as a prophet. It's not that God did not keep the prophetic ministry in the family, but God did allow it to skip a generation. Thus, you might have gifted and anointed children who will faithfully serve in ministry but may not be called to pastor the church. However, this does not eliminate the possibility that a grandson or granddaughter, someone of a next, or another generation, will not pick up the prophetic or pastoral gift[37], and lead the congregation in the future. It might still be your son, but your son, once removed.

---

[37] A notable contemporary example of this would be Apostle Herman Murry who became the pastor of Full Gospel Holy Temple in Dallas, Texas and presiding bishop of the Full Gospel Holy Temple Churches after the passing of his grandfather, Apostle Lobias Murray, in 2011.

"Then the prophet, Haggai the prophet, and Zechariah the son of Iddo, prophesied unto the Jews that were in Judah and Jerusalem in the name of the God of Israel, even unto them" (Ezra 5:1 KJV).

To add to this section, one might be childless, but like Abraham (at the time) have the responsibility to care for a nephew like Lot (Read Genesis 12:5); or might be like Mordecai with a cousin like Esther that you have the responsibility to raise (See Esther 2:7). God may have given you an influential, if not essential, role in the life of a cousin or nephew, for them to become successful in life and in ministry. While not necessarily your biological child, they become like a son or daughter to you. Granted, neither Esther nor Lot inherited anything from their family members, but Abraham and Mordecai were critical to their success and survival. In the end, God might still "keep it in the family" even if it is through a grandchild, niece/nephew, or other family member.

JESUS AND HIS MOTHER: MARY

"In the sixth month of Elizabeth's pregnancy, God sent the angel Gabriel to Nazareth, a town in Galilee, to a virgin pledged to be married to a man named Joseph, a descendant of David. The virgin's name was Mary. The angel went to her and said, "Greetings, you who are highly favored! The Lord is with you."

Mary was greatly troubled at his words and wondered what kind of greeting this might be. But the angel said to her, "Do not be afraid, Mary; you have found favor with God. You will conceive and give birth to a son, and you are to call him Jesus. He will be great and will be called the Son of the Most High. The Lord God will give him the throne of his father David, [33] and he will reign over Jacob's descendants forever; his kingdom will never end."

"How will this be," Mary asked the angel, "since I am a virgin?" The angel answered, "The Holy Spirit will come on you, and the power of the Most High will overshadow you. So, the holy one to be born will be called the Son of God. Even Elizabeth your relative is going to have a

118

child in her old age, and she who was said to be unable to conceive is in her sixth month. For no word from God will ever fail." "I am the Lord's servant," Mary answered. "May your word to me be fulfilled." Then the angel left her. (Luke 1: 26-38 NIV)

"While Jesus was still talking to the crowd, his mother and brothers stood outside, wanting to speak to him. Someone told him, "Your mother and brothers are standing outside, wanting to speak to you." He replied to him, "Who is my mother, and who are my brothers?" Pointing to his disciples, he said, "Here are my mother and my brothers. For whoever does the will of my Father in heaven is my brother and sister and mother." (Matthew 12:46-50, NIV)

'When they arrived, they went upstairs to the room where they were staying. Those present were Peter, John, James and Andrew; Philip and Thomas, Bartholomew and Matthew; James son of Alphaeus and Simon the Zealot, and Judas son of James. They all joined together constantly in prayer, along with the women and Mary the mother of Jesus, and with his brothers. In those days Peter stood up among the believers (a group numbering about a hundred and twenty)" (Acts 1: 12-15, NIV).

Once again, this passage is not intended to argue anything about the role of women in the church. However, it should be noted that if anyone would have been qualified to replace Judas as one of the 12 apostles, it would have been Mary, the mother of Jesus! Yet, as Scripture records, Mary was one of the 120 in the Upper Room. It is not recorded that Mary asserted herself or took on any leadership position in the early church. However, Jesus did ask his disciples from the cross to take care of his mother.[38] Further, the Scripture does not even suggest that Mary sought

---

[38] "Now there stood by the cross of Jesus his mother, and his mother's sister, Mary the wife of Cleophas, and Mary Magdalene. When Jesus therefore saw his mother, and the disciple standing by, whom he loved, he saith unto his mother, Woman, behold thy son! Then saith he to the disciple, Behold thy mother! And from that hour that disciple took her unto his own home" (John 19:25-27 KJV).

any special treatment, recognition, title, position, or memorialization in the early church. In fact, after Acts chapter 1, Mary is not mentioned anymore in the New Testament. If Mary, the mother of Jesus, can remain humble and respect who Jesus left in charge of the church, surely, she has established a standard for all parents to follow!

On the contrary, there are moments where a parent may need to take a more active role in the succession plan or process. A spouse or parent should not interfere or dictate their preference when there is a documented succession plan in place. However, if the plan is vague or misunderstood, a parent or spouse can bring clarity to an otherwise murky situation. For example, Bathsheba was required to assert herself into the succession process because David had not made his decision public. Moreover, without question, the wife of a former king, or the mother of a future king, should be honored and respected. Solomon honored his mother, Bathsheba, with a seat next to his (I Kings 2:19).[39] Hence, honor is earned not assumed; nor should it be taken, but given.

CLOSING

God may or may not continue a legacy through sons. God may use a daughter or grandson. God may also disqualify children because of their unrighteousness and unethical behavior. The key takeaway from this chapter is not to force something that you want when it is not God's will. It may cause more harm to them, your family, your church, and your legacy to have the wrong person succeed you. Rather than make your name last in the earth, they may be the reason it gets tarnished or extinguished. In Chapter 9, we will further explore some cases where the consequences outweigh the benefit when it comes to having a child placed on the throne.

---

[39] Asa, however, removed his grandmother, queen mother Maachach, from her special seat because of her idolatry (II Chronicles 15:16).

QUESTIONS FOR REFLECTION

1. How would you access or explain the relationship between Moses and his sons, Gershom and Eleazar? How can leaders prevent having their children resent or reject the ministry?

2. Why do you think Eli failed to correct his sons, even after being warned twice about their behavior and God's judgment against them?

3. How can a leader prevent allowing love to make them blind when it comes to the flaws and failings of their children?

4. How can fathers help their daughters find their place in the organization (i.e. church, ministry, business, etc.) and prepare them to be the successor to an organization?

5. What should be the role of parents and spouses in creating or implementing a succession plan?

CHAPTER 9
MANTLES THAT FELL AND FAILED

A FAILED TRANSFER

This chapter will examine five transitions in leadership. In each case, the successor made poor choices that negatively impacted their administration. However, the total blame for the successor's failure did not solely rest on their shoulders. It was the actions of the predecessor that predetermined the fate and failure of the next leader.

JOSHUA AND THE JUDGES

"Then Joshua told the people they could go home. So, each one went to take his own share of the land. The people of Israel served the Lord as long as Joshua was alive. They continued serving the Lord during the lifetimes of the elders who lived on after Joshua. These men had seen all the great things the Lord had done for Israel. Joshua son of Nun was the servant of the Lord. Joshua died at the age of 110. So, the Israelites buried him in the land he had been given. That land was at Timnath Heres. It was in the mountains of Ephraim, north of Mount Gaash. After those people had died, their children grew up. They did not know the Lord or what he had done for Israel" (Judges 2:6-10 ICB).

The Scripture informs us that after the death of Joshua, Israel was left in the hand of a group of elders. Perhaps these elders were those under the age of 20 who were old enough to witness everything God did through Moses in Egypt and in the wilderness. For the first time the people were left without a leader such as Moses, Aaron, Joshua, Caleb, or Eleazar. Consequently, they served God for one generation after Joshua. However, there arose a generation that did not know God. As a result, the people opted to do what was right in their own eyes. Cycles of anarchy, idolatry, bondage, repentance, and restoration would follow intermittently for the next 300 years.

Judges 2:11-15 (KJV) records, "And the children of Israel did evil in the sight of the Lord, and served Baalim: And they forsook the Lord God of their fathers, which brought them out of the land of Egypt, and followed other gods, of the gods of the people that were round about them, and bowed themselves unto them, and provoked the Lord to anger. And they forsook the Lord and served Baal and Ashtaroth. And the anger of the Lord was hot against Israel, and he delivered them into the hands of spoilers that spoiled them, and he sold them into the hands of their enemies roundabout, so that they could not any longer stand before their enemies. Whithersoever they went out, the hand of the Lord was against them for evil, as the Lord had said, and as the Lord had sworn unto them: and they were greatly distressed."

During these 300 years, Israel would lack consistent civil, military, or religious leadership. The tribes fought their own battles, and at times, turned against each other. Many of the inhabitants were never driven out of the land as God had commanded. They often made regrettable alliances with other nations against the will of God. The people engaged in unauthorized marriages with pagan worshippers. As the Scripture says, the people "worship worthless idols and became worthless themselves" (Jeremiah 2:5 NIV).

One could argue that to appoint someone else to lead would have been the equivalent of establishing a monarchy. Gideon affirms this premise when he declared, "And Gideon said unto them, I will not rule over you, neither shall my son rule over you: the LORD shall rule over you" (Judges 8:23). Yet if God did not want Israel to have a leader, why did God always raise judges to deliver and lead the people? Over 300 years, God would use 11 judges to lead and govern Israel. Could a council of elders have been established to provide unity and oversight for the new nation?

Did God intend for Israel to suffer anarchy as a result of not having an established monarchy?

Regardless of the reason why Joshua did not appoint a successor, there is little disagreement that its failure led Israel to becoming a mess very quickly. Therefore, the question must be asked: should Joshua have done more to leave some type of leadership structure or succession plan in place? If God gave Joshua to Moses to lead the people, why didn't Joshua follow the same pattern and ask God for a leader to care for the people after his death?

Moreover, it is important to place Joshua's final words under greater scrutiny. Before his death, Joshua does give the nation a final charge and implores them to serve God. We even celebrate Joshua's emphatic declaration, "As for me and my house we will serve the Lord!" However, on a second reading, was Joshua being selfish in his statement? Was it really a declaration of his faith in God or was it more of a statement, "me and mine are good, you can make your own decision as to what you want to do after I'm gone?"; perhaps even a "drop the mic" moment for Joshua. After serving and holding a "leadership position" in Israel for almost 70 years (40 with Moses and 30 of his own), Joshua may have been simply tired.

Thus, even if a leader is not in a position to select a successor, it is important that the leader does what they can to help ensure that the culture and structure is in place for the congregation to succeed in the future. Moses did not have a succession plan until he knew he was getting ready to die. Moreover, Moses did not have a successor until he asked God specifically who would lead the people after he passed away.

The Scripture does not record where Joshua ever asked God what should be done next. Thus, it is also important to seek God for selecting a successor or in developing a succession plan. If God instructs a leader to "leave it alone" then it will also be God's responsibility to "raise up a judge" to lead the people in the future (See Judges 2:16-19).

SAUL AND JONATHAN

"Saul was thirty years old when he became king, and he reigned over Israel forty-two years. Saul chose three thousand men from Israel; two thousand were with him at Michmash and in the hill country of Bethel, and a thousand were with Jonathan at Gibeah in Benjamin. The rest of the men he sent back to their homes.

Jonathan attacked the Philistine outpost at Geba, and the Philistines heard about it. Then Saul had the trumpet blown throughout the land and said, "Let the Hebrews hear!" So, all Israel heard the news: "Saul has attacked the Philistine outpost, and now Israel has become obnoxious to the Philistines." And the people were summoned to join Saul at Gilgal.

The Philistines assembled to fight Israel, with three thousand chariots, six thousand charioteers, and soldiers as numerous as the sand on the seashore. They went up and camped at Michmash, east of Beth Aven. When the Israelites saw that their situation was critical and that their army was hard pressed, they hid in caves and thickets, among the rocks, and in pits and cisterns. Some Hebrews even crossed the Jordan to the land of Gad and Gilead.

Saul remained at Gilgal, and all the troops with him were quaking with fear. He waited seven days, the time set by Samuel; but Samuel did not come to Gilgal, and Saul's men began to scatter. So, he said, "Bring me the burnt offering and the fellowship offerings." And Saul offered up the burnt offering. Just as he finished making the offering, Samuel arrived, and Saul went out to greet him.

"What have you done?" asked Samuel. Saul replied, "When I saw that the men were scattering, and that you did not come at the set time, and that the Philistines were assembling at Michmash, I thought, 'Now the Philistines will come down against me at Gilgal, and I have not sought the LORD's favor.' So, I felt compelled to offer the burnt offering."

"You have done a foolish thing," Samuel said. "You have not kept the command the LORD your God gave you; if you had, he would have established your kingdom over Israel for all time. But now your kingdom will not endure; the LORD has sought out a man after his own heart and appointed him ruler of his people, because you have not kept the LORD's command." I Samuel 13:1-15 (NIV)

"Samuel said to Saul, "I am the one the LORD sent to anoint you king over his people Israel; so, listen now to the message from the LORD. This is what the LORD Almighty says: 'I will punish the Amalekites for what they did to Israel when they waylaid them as they came up from Egypt. Now go, attack the Amalekites and totally destroy all that belongs to them. Do not spare them; put to death men and women, children and infants, cattle and sheep, camels and donkeys.'"

Then Saul attacked the Amalekites all the way from Havilah to Shur, near the eastern border of Egypt. He took Agag, king of the Amalekites alive, and all his people he totally destroyed with the sword. But Saul and the army spared Agag and the best of the sheep and cattle, the fat calves and lambs—everything that was good. They were unwilling to destroy completely, but everything that was despised and weak they totally destroyed.

Then the word of the LORD came to Samuel: "I regret that I have made Saul king, because he has turned away from me and has not carried out my instructions." Samuel was angry, and he cried out to the LORD all that night.

Samuel said, "Although you were once small in your own eyes, did you not become the head of the tribes of Israel? The LORD anointed you king over Israel. And he sent you on a mission, saying, 'Go and completely destroy those wicked people, the Amalekites; wage war against them until you have wiped them out.' Why did you not obey the LORD? Why did you pounce on the plunder and do evil in the eyes of the LORD?"

But Samuel replied: "Does the LORD delight in burnt offerings and sacrifices as much as in obeying the LORD? To obey is better than sacrifice, and to heed is better than the fat of rams. For rebellion is like the sin of divination, and arrogance like the evil of idolatry. Because you have rejected the word of the LORD, he has rejected you as king."

Then Saul said to Samuel, "I have sinned. I violated the LORD's command and your instructions. I was afraid of the men and so I gave in to them. Now I beg you, forgive my sin and come back with me, so that I may worship the LORD." But Samuel said to him, "I will not go back with you. You have rejected the word of the LORD, and the LORD has rejected you as king over Israel!"

As Samuel turned to leave, Saul caught hold of the hem of his robe, and it tore. Samuel said to him, "The LORD has torn the kingdom of Israel from you today and has given it to one of your neighbors—to one better than you. He who is the Glory of Israel does not lie or change his mind; for he is not a human being, that he should change his mind." (I Samuel 15:1-3 ,7-10, 17-19, 22-29 NIV)

Samuel said, "Why do you consult me, now that the LORD has departed from you and become your enemy? The LORD has done what he predicted through me. The LORD has torn the kingdom out of your hands and given it to one of your neighbors—to David. Because you did not obey the LORD or carry out his fierce wrath against the Amalekites the LORD has done this to you today. The LORD will deliver both Israel and you into the hands of the Philistines, and tomorrow you and your sons will be with me. The LORD will also give the army of Israel into the hands of the Philistines." (I Samuel 28:16-19 NIV)

"Now the Philistines fought against Israel: and the men of Israel fled from before the Philistines and fell down slain in mount Gilboa. And the Philistines followed hard upon Saul and upon his sons; and the Philistines slew Jonathan, and Abinadab, and Melchishua, Saul's sons. So, Saul died, and his three sons, and his armourbearer, and all his men, that same day together." (I Samuel 31:1-2 KJV)

God promised Saul that he would establish his reign as king over Israel. However, because of a willingness to capitulate to the people; become jealous of his greatest asset, David; disobey, and the lie about destroying the Amalekites - God took the kingdom away from Saul and gave it to David. Not only did Saul die because of his sins, but also his heir to

128

the throne, Jonathan[40], was robbed of his chance at becoming the next king of Israel. Saul tried to blame David for Jonathan's missed opportunity to be king; but it was Saul's own doing that led to Jonathan, and his two other sons, being murdered by the Philistines.

Not only did Saul's disobedience cause three of his children to be killed at the hands of Philistines, but his unethical behavior led to the death of seven more of his sons. II Samuel 21 records a three-year famine in the land. David inquires of the Lord who revealed to him "it is for Saul, and for his bloody house, because he slew the Gibeonites." Years after Saul's death, the nation was still suffering because of his disobedience, poor decisions, and failed leadership. To make atonement for Saul breaking a 400-year vow with the Gibeonites, the Gibeonites demanded that seven of Saul's sons be delivered to them and hung for Saul's offense.[41]

Sadly, the only good thing that came out of the massacre of Saul's seven sons is that it caused Saul and his sons, including Jonathan, to have a proper burial in Saul's homeland of Benjamin. Saul disobedience not only got him killed, but a total of 10 of his sons. God forbid if any of our life's decisions causes the death or destruction of any of our children! Learn the lesson from Saul – "to obey is better than sacrifice, and to hearken than the fat of rams"!

SOLOMON AND REHOBOAM

"King Solomon was greater in riches and wisdom than all the other kings of the earth" (II Chronicles 9:22 NIV).

"When Solomon had finished building the temple of the LORD and the royal palace, and had achieved all he had desired to do, the LORD appeared to him a second time, as he had appeared to him at Gibeon. The LORD said to him: "I have heard the prayer and plea you have

---

[40] "For as long as the son of Jesse liveth upon the ground, thou shalt not be established, nor thy kingdom. Wherefore now send and fetch him unto me, for he shall surely die." (I Samuel 20:31 KJV)

[41] Spared from the hanging was Mephibosheth, the son of Jonathan, because the oath between David and Jonathan. (II Samuel 21:7).

made before me; I have consecrated this temple, which you have built, by putting my Name there forever. My eyes and my heart will always be there.

"As for you, if you walk before me faithfully with integrity of heart and uprightness, as David your father did, and do all I command and observe my decrees and laws, I will establish your royal throne over Israel forever, as I promised David your father when I said, 'You shall never fail to have a successor on the throne of Israel' (I Kings 9:1-5 NIV).

When the queen of Sheba heard of Solomon's fame, she came to Jerusalem to test him with hard questions. Arriving with a very great caravan—with camels carrying spices, large quantities of gold, and precious stones—she came to Solomon and talked with him about all she had on her mind. Solomon answered all her questions; nothing was too hard for him to explain to her. When the queen of Sheba saw he wisdom of Solomon, as well as the palace he had built, the food on his table, the seating of his officials, the attending servants in their robes, the cupbearers in their robes and the burnt offerings he made at the temple of the LORD, she was overwhelmed.

She said to the king, "The report I heard in my own country about your achievements and your wisdom is true. But I did not believe what they said until I came and saw with my own eyes. Indeed, not even half the greatness of your wisdom was told me; you have far exceeded the report I heard. How happy your people must be! How happy your officials, who continually stand before you and hear your wisdom! Praise be to the LORD your God, who has delighted in you and placed you on his throne as king to rule for the LORD your God. Because of the love of your God for Israel and his desire to uphold them forever, he has made you king over them, to maintain justice and righteousness" (I Chronicles 9:1-8 NIV).

Thirty years after becoming the king of Israel, Solomon had completed erecting the temple and his own palace. Solomon enjoyed peace throughout the kingdom. His wealth, wisdom, fortune, and fame were known throughout the world. Indeed, King Solomon had "passed all the kings of the earth in riches and wisdom" (I Kings 9:22 KJV). The Queen of Sheba confirmed it when she exclaimed, "Howbeit I believed not the words, until I came, and mine eyes had seen it: and, behold, the half was not told me: thy wisdom and prosperity exceedeth the fame which I heard" (I Kings 10:7 KJV).

With the covenant God had made with Solomon and the promises God had fulfilled in Solomon's life, Solomon allowed "strange women" to turn his heart away from God. Solomon built shrines and sacrificed to false god in order to appease his many wives. God became so angry with Solomon, that God declared He would "rend" or tear the kingdom away from Solomon and give it to another man.

"And Solomon did evil in the sight of the LORD, and went not fully after the LORD, as did David his father...And the LORD was angry with Solomon, because his heart was turned from the LORD God of Israel, which had appeared unto him twice, And had commanded him concerning this thing, that he should not go after other gods: but he kept not that which the LORD commanded. Wherefore the LORD said unto Solomon, Forasmuch as this is done of thee, and thou hast not kept my covenant and my statutes, which I have commanded thee, I will surely rend the kingdom from thee, and will give it to thy servant" (I Kings 11:6, 9-11 KJV).

When reading this passage, one can understand God's frustration and disappointment in Solomon. After all God had done for Solomon and the numerous warnings Solomon had received from God; Solomon would turn around and betray God by worshiping other deities. God in his judgment declares He will take the kingdom from Solomon and give it to another man. Yet in God's mercy, he would not split the kingdom during Solomon's lifetime.

"Wherefore the LORD said unto Solomon, Forasmuch as this is done of thee, and thou hast not kept my covenant and my statutes, which I have commanded thee, I will surely rend the kingdom from thee, and will give it to thy servant. Notwithstanding in thy days I will not do it for David thy father's sake: but I will rend it out of the hand of thy son. Howbeit I will

131

not rend away all the kingdom; but will give one tribe to thy son for David my servant's sake, and for Jerusalem's sake which I have chosen" (I King 11:11-13 KJV).

"But I will rend it out of the hand of thy son." The Scripture declares that the son would no longer be subject to punishment based on one's father's behavior. However, in God's judgment, Solomon is spared the consequences of his action, but his son, Rehoboam, would bear it completely. Granted, Rehoboam made a major blunder as a newly inaugurated king; when asked by the people to alleviate their taxes and workload. Rehoboam chose to follow the advice of his childhood friends over the advice of his father's advisors. As a result, ten tribes rebelled against Rehoboam and succeeded from the nation.

The Book of II Chronicles gives a slightly different interpretation of the matter than the Book of I Kings, indicting Rehoboam because he "forsook the law of the Lord" and "he did evil, because he prepared not his heart to seek the Lord" (II Chronicles 12:1, 14 KJV). Even with Rehoboam humbling himself and repenting later in life, the consequence of Rehoboam's decision was predetermined by the conduct of his father, Solomon. The Scripture informs us,

"So, Jeroboam and all the people came to Rehoboam the third day, as the king had appointed, saying, Come to me again the third day. And the king answered the people roughly, and forsook the old men's counsel that they gave him; And spake to them after the counsel of the young men, saying, My father made your yoke heavy, and I will add to your yoke: my father also chastised you with whips, but I will chastise you with scorpions. Wherefore the king hearkened not unto the people; for the cause was from the LORD, that he might perform his saying, which the LORD spake by Abijah the Shilonite unto Jeroboam the son of Nebat...

Thus, saith the LORD, Ye shall not go up, nor fight against your brethren the children of Israel: return every man to his house; for this thing is from me. They hearkened therefore to the word of the LORD, and returned to depart, according to the word of the LORD" (I King 12:12-15, 24 KJV).

Thus, a leader has to be careful not to take actions or make decisions that would ensure the moral, financial, managerial, or spiritual failure of their successor. Leaders should set their successor up to succeed, not set them up to fail! David positioned his son, Solomon, to have the most successful reign in Israel's history. However, Solomon, positioned his son, Rehoboam, to have the least successful reign in Israel's history.[42] Are you leaving "Solomon" the legacy of "David" or are leaving "Rehoboam" the legacy of "Solomon"? How you lead now will have a major impact on how the next person will be able to lead in the future. Be a David and not a Solomon!

HEZEKIAH AND MANASSEH

"Hezekiah son of Ahaz began to rule over Judah in the third year of King Hoshea's reign in Israel. He was twenty-five years old when he became king, and he reigned in Jerusalem twenty-nine years. His mother was Abijah, the daughter of Zechariah. He did what was pleasing in the LORD's sight, just as his ancestor David had done.

Hezekiah trusted in the LORD, the God of Israel. There was no one like him among all the kings of Judah, either before or after his time. He remained faithful to the LORD in everything, and he carefully obeyed all the commands the LORD had given Moses. So, the LORD was with him, and Hezekiah was successful in everything he did. He revolted against the king of Assyria and refused to pay him tribute" (II Kings 18:1-3, 5-7 NLT).

"And Hezekiah received the letter of the hand of the messengers and read it: and Hezekiah went up into the house of the LORD AND spread it before the LORD. Then Isaiah the son of Amoz sent to Hezekiah, saying, thus saith the LORD God of Israel, that which thou hast prayed to me against Sennacherib king of Assyria I have heard. And it came to pass that night, that the angel of the LORD went out, and smote in the camp of the Assyrians

---

[42] Other kings may have led Israel to backslide and eventually into bondage, but no other king had the legacy of causing Israel to become a divided nation.

an hundred fourscore and five thousand: and when they arose early in the morning, behold, they were all dead corpses" (II Kings 19:14, 20, 35 KJV).

"In those days was Hezekiah sick unto death. And the prophet Isaiah the son of Amoz came to him, and said unto him, thus saith the LORD, set thine house in order; for thou shalt die, and not live. Then he turned his face to the wall, and prayed unto the LORD, saying, I beseech thee, O LORD, remember now how I have walked before thee in truth and with a perfect heart, and have done that which is good in thy sight. And Hezekiah wept sore.

And it came to pass, afore Isaiah was gone out into the middle court, that the word of the LORD came to him, saying, Turn again, and tell Hezekiah the captain of my people, Thus saith the LORD, the God of David thy father, I have heard thy prayer, I have seen thy tears: behold, I will heal thee: on the third day thou shalt go up unto the house of the LORD. And I will add unto thy days fifteen years; and I will deliver thee and this city out of the hand of the king of Assyria; and I will defend this city for mine own sake, and for my servant David's sake" (II Kings 20:1-6 KJV).

"At that time Merodachbaladan, the son of Baladan, king of Babylon, sent letters and a present to Hezekiah: for he had heard that he had been sick, and was recovered. And Hezekiah was glad of them, and shewed them the house of his precious things, the silver, and the gold, and the spices, and the precious ointment, and all the house of his armour, and all that was found in his treasures: there was nothing in his house, nor in all his dominion, that Hezekiah shewed them not.

Then came Isaiah the prophet unto king Hezekiah, and said unto him, what said these men? and from whence came they unto thee? And Hezekiah said, they are come from a far country unto me, even from Babylon. Then said he, what have they seen in thine house? And Hezekiah answered, all that is in mine house have they seen: there is nothing among my treasures that I have not shewed them.

Then said Isaiah to Hezekiah, Hear the word of the LORD of hosts: Behold, the days come, that all that is in thine house, and that which thy fathers have laid up in store until this day, shall be carried to Babylon: nothing shall be left, saith the LORD. And of thy sons that shall issue from thee, which thou shalt beget, shall they take away; and they shall be eunuchs in the palace of the king of Babylon.

Then said Hezekiah to Isaiah, Good is the word of the LORD which thou hast spoken. He said moreover, for there shall be peace and truth in my days" (Isaiah 39:1-8 KJV).

Unquestionably, King Hezekiah is considered one of the most successful and revered kings of Israel's history. As an administrator, Hezekiah is credited for building the Siloam or Hezekiah's Tunnel; a-state-of-the-art irrigation system that brought water into Jerusalem (II Kings 20:20; II Chronicles 32:30). Militarily, Hezekiah prevailed over the Assyrian army without a single fight. Spiritually, Hezekiah reinstituted the Passover, inviting people from both Judah and the 10 northern tribes of Israel to participate. The Scripture records that the Passover had never been celebrated on that magnitude since the time of King David. Hezekiah renovated the temple, reinstituted tithing to support the priest, Levites, and their families. By every account, Hezekiah was the man!

However, the Scripture records that with all of Hezekiah's success, pride began to set in with his heart.

"In those days Hezekiah was sick to the death and prayed unto the LORD: and he spake unto him, and he gave him a sign. But Hezekiah rendered not again according to the benefit done unto him; for his heart was lifted up: therefore, there was wrath upon him, and upon Judah and Jerusalem. Notwithstanding Hezekiah humbled himself for the pride of his heart, both he and the inhabitants of Jerusalem, so that the wrath of the LORD came not upon them in the days of Hezekiah" (II Chronicles 32:24-26 KJV).

Yet because Hezekiah humbled himself with tears asking God to remember how he had walked before God and kept his commandments; God healed him and extended his life by 15 years. Sadly, the spirit of pride overcame Hezekiah again. This time in the form of flaunting his wealth to

Babylonian guests as if his wealth were by his own doings. "Howbeit in the business of the ambassadors of the prince of Babylon, who sent unto him to inquire of the wonder that was done in the land, God left him, to try him, that he might know all that was in his heart" (II Chronicles 32:31 KJV).

Again, the prophet Isaiah has to rebuke Hezekiah. However, this time, Isaiah prophesied that the treasure would be taken by the Babylonians and that his sons would be sold into slavery. Any leader should cringe at Hezekiah's reply, "for there shall be peace and truth in my days" (II Kings 20:19; Isaiah 39:8). In other words, Hezekiah said, "ok, good, I don't care, so long as it doesn't happen during my lifetime!" What?!

How can any great leader be so callous and indifferent when it comes to the next generation? So long as it doesn't happen on my watch, my lifetime or during my administration - I don't care! The Scripture later indicates that during the 15 "bonus years" of Hezekiah's that he gave birth to Manasseh, the most wicked king in the history of Israel! Jeremiah 15:4 (KJV) declares, "And I will cause them to be removed into all kingdoms of the earth, because of Manasseh the son of Hezekiah king of Judah, for that which he did in Jerusalem."

Yes, Manasseh was "his own man" and made his own mistakes. Yet, consequently, it was Hezekiah's actions, pride, and indifference that led Israel to completely backslide from all of the revivals and reforms that he had initiated during his tenure. Three places in the Bible (II Kings, II Chronicles, and Isaiah) the blame for Israel's troubles is placed squarely on the shoulders of Hezekiah. Don't let your legacy be tainted because of pride, apathy, bitterness, or resentment. God forbid if any leader has the attitude, "I don't care what happens when I'm gone!" What you do, and how you lead, not only affects you, but may very well predetermine the outcome of the future.

ZEDEKIAH AND HIS SONS

"Zedekiah was 21 years old when he became king. And he was king in Jerusalem for 11 years. His mother's name was Hamutal daughter of Jeremiah, from Libnah. Zedekiah did what the Lord said was wrong, just as Jehoiakim had done. All this happened in Jerusalem and Judah because the Lord was angry with them. Finally, he threw them out of his presence. Zedekiah turned against the king of Babylon.

But the Babylonian army chased King Zedekiah. They caught up with him in the plains of Jericho. All of his army was scattered from him. So, they captured Zedekiah and took him to the king of Babylon at Riblah; there he passed sentence on Zedekiah. There at Riblah the king of Babylon killed Zedekiah's sons as he watched. The king also killed all the officers of Judah. Then he put out Zedekiah's eyes. He put bronze chains on him and took him to Babylon. And the king kept Zedekiah in prison there until the day he died" Jeremiah 52:1-11 ICB)

Imagine, the last thing that you see with your eyes is your sons being slain in front of you. Moreover, imagine the feeling when you know it is all your fault or could have been prevented. This is the story of Zedekiah, the last king of Israel. The Scripture records that Zedekiah was twenty-one when he became king. Zedekiah opted to do "that which was evil in the eyes of the Lord" (Jeremiah 52:2). Zedekiah was so conflicted as a leader that on one hand he would imprison Jeremiah because of Jeremiah's prophecies. Yet on the other hand, Zedekiah would sneak into the prison to visit Jeremiah and receive instructions from him.

After a four-month siege of Jerusalem by the Babylonian, Zedekiah rejected Jeremiah's admonition to surrender. Zedekiah decided rather to flee, along with his family from Jerusalem to Jericho. It is there that Nebuchadnezzar, king of Babylon, executes judgment upon Zedekiah and his sons. Zedekiah's sons are slain in front of him before Nebuchadnezzar gouges out his eyes.

Similar to Saul, Zedekiah's legacy is cut short and his sons are slain because of his rebellion and unwillingness to obey God. Yet, unlike Saul, who would die in battle with his sons, Zedekiah would have to live the rest of his life with the guilt, regret, and images of his sons being slain before him because of his decision. Every day, for the rest of Zedekiah's life, he would have to hear the words of Jeremiah's warning and the shrills of his sons being murdered. God forbid that our legacy, or more importantly the lives of our children are cut short because of our own sins. Saul and Zedekiah had no one to pick up their "mantles when they fell" because the ones who could have caught them were dead.

Prayerfully, you will never experience your children actually being slain before your eyes. However, a leader's conduct can lead to a child being slain mentally, emotionally, and spiritually. Don't allow your ego, ambition, pride, disobedience, immorality or misplaced priorities, be the cause of your child not being in the position to receive your mantle when it falls. If you are Zedekiah, I urge you to turn back, please turn back, before it is too late! Even if our children should stray away, let it not be because you push them away or lead them astray. God forbid!

SUMMATION

In closing, for these five relationships, we learn that the failure of the next generation was predetermined due to failures from the previous generation. Joshua neglected to place anyone in charge of Israel and as a result they "did what was right in their own eyes." Saul's disobedience caused 10 of his sons to be killed and for another man to succeed him. Solomon backslid and worshipped other gods. As a result, God would take 10 of the 12 tribes away from his son, Rehoboam. Hezekiah allowed pride and indifference to creep into his life. His lack of concern for the future caused him to produce a son that would be labeled as the most wicked in history. Zedekiah's failure to follow the instructions of the prophet, led to his sons being killed right before his eyes. Indeed, the future will determine how the past is evaluated!

QUESTIONS FOR REFLECTION
1. Why do you think Joshua did not place someone in charge of Israel before his death?

2. Why do you think Hezekiah became so indifferent to the future?
3. How can leaders avoid being blinded or misguided by pride?
4. Why does God allow future leaders to suffer the consequence of mistakes made by previous leaders? In what ways are you not yielding to the voice of God today, that could cause problems for your congregation in the future?
5. How can a current leader correct a past mistake before it negatively impacts a future leader?
6. Saul (Samuel), Hezekiah (Isaiah), and Zedekiah (Jeremiah) all had prophets in their lives to warn and instruct them in the ways of God. How important is it for a leader to have a "prophet" in their life to advise and hold them accountable with God?

CHAPTER 10
PREPARING THE PROTÉGÉ TO PROSPER:
7 TIPS TO PREPARING A SUCCESSOR

1. BE PROACTIVE WITH SUCCESSION PLANNING

The question often asked is when should a leader start planning for succession. While on one hand the answer can be complex, on the other hand, it is very simple – day one! One should essentially begin the process of working oneself out of a job or leadership position on the first day of taking the position. Robert Griener provides this career and leadership advice, [43]

"Whatever job position you find yourself in, you should always be trying to work yourself out of a job. In a nutshell, working yourself out of a job means building up your team in such a way that someday you could walk away from your project and everything would continue running normally without a hitch. In order to do this, you must invest greatly in your team. You must push and inspire them to grow and improve their skill set. You must keep them from becoming demotivated and complacent."

Thus, even if there is no formal plan, mentorship program, or identified successor in place, a leader should focus on building strong

---

[43] Points derived from "Preparing for Succession Planning" by Bishop Michael W. Fields, You Can Get There From Here: Pastors and Visionaries Conference, Friday, October 31, 2019, Atlanta, Georgia. For additional information read, "What is Succession Planning? Your steps to success" https://www.roberthalf.com/blog/management-tips/7-steps-to-building-a-succession-plan-for-success and https://www.roberthalf.co.uk/advice/human-resource-management/what-succession-planning-your-steps-success retrieved June 13, 2020.

teams that consist of individuals that can be groomed into future leadership positions. This is especially true in the church. Jesus instructs his followers to make or produce more disciples. In turn, disciples should mature and reproduce more disciples. Thus, in a church, a pastor should be producing other believers, disciples, ministers, and leaders that can grow and contribute even more to the ministry, moreover the Kingdom of God, in the future.

It starts with simply being a role model of leadership that others can pattern after and strive to become in the future. The fruit doesn't fall far from the tree. Thus, a pastor cannot expect to have a great batch of leaders to work with in the future, if they have not planted the seeds of good leadership in their garden.

Further expounding upon the analogy of a tree, most trees do not grow up and produce quality fruit overnight. It takes time! Thus, the earlier a leader starts planting, the earlier the leader can reap a harvest. It's one thing to tell you how to lead; it's another thing to show you how to lead. Be the leader that you would want to follow!

2. KEEP AN OPEN MIND

Robert Half writes, "While the obvious successor may be the second in command, don't disregard other promising employees. Look for people who best display the skills necessary to thrive in higher positions, regardless of their current title."

When it was time to select deacons for the early church, the apostles did not select them, but gave the criteria to the people to select them.

"Wherefore, brethren, look ye out among you seven men of honest report, full of the Holy Ghost and wisdom, whom we may appoint over this business... And the saying pleased the whole multitude: and they chose Stephen, a man full of faith and of the Holy Ghost, and Philip, and Prochorus, and Nicanor, and Timon, and Parmenas, and Nicolas a proselyte of Antioch:" (Acts 6:3, 5-6 KJV)

142

Who can forget what God said to Samuel after being sent to Jessie's house to find a replacement for Saul?

"The LORD said to Samuel, "How long will you mourn for Saul, since I have rejected him as king over Israel? Fill your horn with oil and be on your way; I am sending you to Jesse of Bethlehem. I have chosen one of his sons to be king." But Samuel said, "How can I go? If Saul hears about it, he will kill me." The LORD said, "Take a heifer with you and say, 'I have come to sacrifice to the LORD.' Invite Jesse to the sacrifice, and I will show you what to do. You are to anoint for me the one I indicate."

When they arrived, Samuel saw Eliab and thought, "Surely the LORD's anointed stands here before the LORD." But the LORD said to Samuel, "Do not consider his appearance or his height, for I have rejected him. The LORD does not look at the things people look at. People look at the outward appearance, but the LORD looks at the heart." Then Jesse called Abinadab and had him pass in front of Samuel. But Samuel said, "The LORD has not chosen this one either." Jesse then had Shammah pass by, but Samuel said, "Nor has the LORD chosen this one." Jesse had seven of his sons pass before Samuel, but Samuel said to him, "The LORD has not chosen these." So, he asked Jesse, "Are these all the sons you have?" "There is still the youngest," Jesse answered. "He is tending the sheep." Samuel said, "Send for him; we will not sit down until he arrives."

So, he sent for him and had him brought in. He was glowing with health and had a fine appearance and handsome features. Then the LORD said, "Rise and anoint him; this is the one." So, Samuel took the horn of oil and anointed him in the presence of his brothers, and from that day on the Spirit of the LORD came powerfully upon David. Samuel then went to Ramah"(I Samuel 16:1-13 KJV).

A leader may have their own desires, plans, and favorites to place in positions of leadership in the church. However, there could be a David out in the field, not fully groomed, minding his own business that God has anointed to be the next pastor or leader of the church. Be open and obedient to the voice of God. Don't miss your David because you are in haste to anoint an Eliab or Abinadab; when God has not authorized you to pour the oil on them!

3. MAKE THE VISION KNOWN

"Include potential managers in strategy conversations to help them acquire planning and leadership skills, as well as a broad vision of the organization and its objectives. Consider sharing your succession planning with human resources and your board of directors."

The New American Standard Bible translates Habakkuk 2:2 this way, "Then the LORD answered me and said, "Record the vision and inscribe it on tablets, That the one who reads it may run." Thus three questions, (1) do you have a vision from God; (2) how have you made it known to the people; and (3) who can you rely on to read it and run with it?

An individual that can not only catch the vision, but contribute, expand, or embellish and implement it, is essential for the success and long-term viability of any church or organization. Moreover, in order for people to catch the vision, they may have to see the vision. This is not in a mystical or metaphorical sense, but by actually taking your team on a field trip or conference where they can see, and experience things done on a different level. Even with the best vocabulary, it may be difficult to articulate or convey a vision to someone who has not seen what you have seen. Sometimes showing a vision is better than telling a vision.

Elijah asked God to open the eyes of the servant to see "the cloud the size of a man's hand" that would produce rain to end a three-year famine (I Kings 18:44). Elisha prayed for his servant, "Lord open his eyes, that he may see. And the Lord opened the eyes of the young man: and he saw: and behold the mountain was full of horses and chariots of fire" surrounding them and ready to defend them" (II Kings 6:15-17). Understand, one cannot be frustrated with people not supporting or following a vision if they cannot see it. Further, a vision that is constantly changing, never emphasized, or lacks structure or a strategic plan to implement, will never be taken seriously by others. A vision must be more than a slogan, a banner, or a picture on the wall. It must be conveyed as a God-given assignment that must be accomplished.

Question: as a pastor-quarterback who do you have running the right pattern, making moves to get free, agile enough to make great catches when you throw them the ball? Prayerfully, you will have a core of receivers that can catch your vision and carry it into the end zone!

4. OFFER REGULAR FEEDBACK TO THE PROTÉGÉ

In her article, "Succession Planning Basics to Master", Geraldine Grones recommends, "When someone uses well-honed presentation skills or outperforms on a project, make note of it. Keep track of these achievements in a top-performer file so you have something to reference the next time a management position opens. Diligently chronicling topics like strong work and achievement will also come in handy during performance reviews." https://www.hcamag.com

One might argue that Jesus was "hard" on his disciples. However, one cannot argue that he did not give them constant feedback. In academia, papers get better because editors give feedback. Athletes get better because coaches give them feedback. Singers get better because instructors give them feedback. Actors get better because directors give them feedback. Teachers get better because administrators give them feedback. Chefs get better because food critics give them feedback. Businesses get better because customers give them feedback. You get the point; one cannot achieve excellence in anything without consistent feedback and a commitment to improve.

So then why is feedback such an issue in the church? Positive, constructive feedback has often been misconstrued as being judgmental, unsupportive, critical, or even the basis for what people label as "church hurt". However, no individual can get better by only hearing someone sing only their praises all the time. In fact, many athletes are motivated by the booze and jeers from the opposing team's fans, rather than from their own cheerleaders.

Paul says it this way, "Let your speech *be* always with grace, seasoned with salt, that ye may know how ye ought to answer every man." If a protégé can't take private feedback from a trusted pastor or mentor, how in the world will they handle the constant unfettered feedback from the congregation? Perhaps their inability to digest seasoned words is an indication that they are not mature enough, at least not yet, to be the next pastor!

5. PROVIDE TRAINING TO PEAK PERFORMERS

"As you identify your top performers, offer mentoring relationships, job shadowing and training, which are true articles of value to help them develop new skills and refine existing ones."

One of the ways to address any identified area of weakness is to provide the individual with training in that particular area. It could come in the form of a book, seminar, conference, apprenticeship, or online course or degree program. This is especially true in the case where, essentially, the individual has great potential, but has weakness or deficiencies that can be addressed. Show them that you are willing to invest in them and their potential by providing training for them. If the individual is not committed to training and improving, then perhaps they are not mature enough, yet to be the next pastor!

6. DO A TRIAL RUN OF YOUR SUCCESSION PLAN

Feedback and training are great, but without trial or application, one will never know the fruit of it. Too often in the church, individuals are promoted before being tested or before they produce fruit. However, Jesus gives a different model for promotion and elevation in the church.

"His lord said unto him, Well done, thou good and faithful servant: thou hast been faithful over a few things, I will make thee ruler over many things: enter thou into the joy of thy lord." (Matthew 25:21 KJV)

Has the protégé proven themselves to be "faithful in the few things" they have been asked to do? Have they ever been given the keys to the

146

car to go out for a test drive? How are they currently demonstrating leadership? How well are they performing as leaders in charge of various auxiliaries, special events, and tasks within the church? How well do they perform when you're not watching, or they think you do not see them?

"Gehazi, the servant of Elisha the man of God, said to himself, "My master was too easy on Naaman, this Aramean, by not accepting from him what he brought. As surely as the LORD lives, I will run after him and get something from him." So Gehazi hurried after Naaman. When Naaman saw him running toward him, he got down from the chariot to meet him. "Is everything all right?" he asked. "Everything is all right," Gehazi answered. "My master sent me to say, 'Two young men from the company of the prophets have just come to me from the hill country of Ephraim. Please give them a talent of silver and two sets of clothing.'"

"By all means, take two talents," said Naaman. He urged Gehazi to accept them, and then tied up the two talents of silver in two bags, with two sets of clothing. He gave them to two of his servants, and they carried them ahead of Gehazi. When Gehazi came to the hill, he took the things from the servants and put them away in the house. He sent the men away and they left."

"When he went in and stood before his master, Elisha asked him, "Where have you been, Gehazi?" "Your servant didn't go anywhere," Gehazi answered. But Elisha said to him, "Was not my spirit with you when the man got down from his chariot to meet you? Is this the time to take money or to accept clothes—or olive groves and vineyards, or flocks and herds, or male and female slaves? Naaman's leprosy will cling to you and to your descendants forever." Then Gehazi went from Elisha's presence and his skin was leprous—it had become as white as snow." (II Kings 5:20-27 NIV).

One of the best ways to test whether a protégé is ready to be the pastor: go away for a period of time and see how they act and the church responds to them. Perhaps a Sunday away for an outside speaking engagement, family vacation, annual leave, foreign missions' trip, or even a sabbatical will provide a different viewpoint for you and the congregation.

"Who then is the faithful and wise servant, whom the master has put in charge of the servants in his household to give them their food at the proper time? It will be good for that servant whose master finds him doing so when he returns. Truly I tell you, he will put him in charge of all his possessions. But suppose that servant is wicked and says to himself, 'My master is staying away a long time,' and he then begins to beat his fellow servants and to eat and drink with drunkards. The master of that servant will come on a day when he does not expect him and at an hour, he is not aware of." (Matthew 24:45-50 NIV)[44]

How many fires do you have to put out when you return or are things in as good, if not better condition, when you return, than when you left it? If every time you go out of town and leave them in charge you have to spend time cleaning up the mess they left behind, perhaps they are not mature enough, yet, to be the next pastor!

7. Use Your Plan to Develop a Hiring Strategy

Once you've identified internal employees as successors for key roles in your organization, take note of any talent gaps. In this way, the succession planning process can help you identify where to focus your recruiting efforts.

To accomplish this, the church must recruit by embracing the prayer of Jesus as recorded in Matthew 9:35-38 (NIV).

"Jesus went through all the towns and villages, teaching in their synagogues, proclaiming the good news of the kingdom and healing every disease and sickness. When he saw the crowds, he had compassion on them, because they were harassed and helpless, like sheep without a shepherd. Then he said to his disciples, "The harvest is plentiful, but the

---

[44] The chapter concludes, "He will cut him to pieces and assign him a place with the hypocrites, where there will be weeping and gnashing of teeth." (Matthew 24:51 NIV) Hopefully you will not have to go this far to reprimand them. However, you might have to cut with words and reassign them to a different area of ministry.

workers are few. Ask the Lord of the harvest, therefore, to send out workers into his harvest field."

When we pray the prayer of Jesus, he will give us the results that Apostle Paul describes in Ephesians 4:12-16 (NIV).

"So Christ himself gave the apostles, the prophets, the evangelists, the pastors and teachers, to equip his people for works of service, so that the body of Christ may be built up until we all reach unity in the faith and in the knowledge of the Son of God and become mature, attaining to the whole measure of the fullness of Christ.

Then we will no longer be infants, tossed back and forth by the waves, and blown here and there by every wind of teaching and by the cunning and craftiness of people in their deceitful scheming. Instead, speaking the truth in love, we will grow to become in every respect the mature body of him who is the head, that is, Christ. From him the whole body, joined and held together by every supporting ligament, grows and builds itself up in love, as each part does its work."

With these seven steps, a church can begin the process of developing a viable succession plan to ensure the continued success of the ministry for decades to come!

QUESTIONS FOR REFLECTION
1. In what ways have you been proactive in succession planning?
2. How much of your church's annual schedule and budget is devoted to leadership training or training for leaders?
3. What are some ways to give consistent and constructive feedback to mentees or potential proteges?
4. What are some ways you can give your succession plan a test run?
5. How do you know if your members know and embrace the vision of the house?

CHAPTER 11
WHO GETS WHAT WHEN I DIE?
CREATING AN ESTATE PLAN FOR YOUR FAMILY

*"DEATH HAS A WAY OF BRINGING PEOPLE CLOSER, JUST TO SEE THEM FALL
OUT AND FIGHT OVER MONEY...SAD!"* ~ BISHOP TROY V. CARTER

"He remembers his covenant forever, the promise he made, for a thousand generations, the covenant he made with Abraham, the oath he swore to Isaac. He confirmed it to Jacob as a decree, to Israel as an everlasting covenant: "To you I will give the land of Canaan as the portion you will inherit."

"For he remembered his holy promise given to his servant Abraham. He brought out his people with rejoicing, his chosen ones with shouts of joy; he gave them the lands of the nations, and they fell heir to what others had toiled for - that they might keep his precepts and observe his laws. Praise the LORD" (PSALMS 105:8-11, 42-45 NIV).

While we celebrate Abraham as the father of our faith, we often overlook the fact that he is also the father of a nation. From Abraham, the children of Israel inherited both faith and fortune. They received a spiritual inheritance which consisted of the revelation of the one and only God. They also received over 5,120,000 acres of land known today as the nation of Israel. A man or woman of God should strive to not only leave behind a legacy of faith, but also an inheritance of wealth!

The purpose of this chapter is to discuss key elements of an estate plan: will, trust and prenuptial agreements. Matters regarding disability and end of life decisions, such as Powers of Attorney, Living Wills, and Health

Care Directives will be discussed in Chapter 12. The topic of life insurance will be discussed in Chapter 14.

WILL

Simply stated, a will is an official written document that allows an individual to determine who, gets what, when the individual passes away. When drafting a will most people often only think of "big-ticket" items or "giving everything" to a spouse or children without any specific instructions about how they should be divided or distributed. Most wills include provisions regarding real estate, business interest, and automobiles.

However, often forgotten and the basis of strife in a family are the smaller, more sentimental items. These items may have less monetary value, but actually have more lasting value to your family. Items such as clothing, jewelry, furniture, family heirlooms, and collector's items may require specific instructions for distribution in a will. Some can recall in 2015, nearly 50 years after his death, that the children of Rev. Dr. Martin Luther King, Jr. were in court fighting over his bible and Nobel Prize! But what do you do with Martin Luther King's bible? Do you keep it and pass it down within the family, archive it in the King Center, place it in a national history museum, or even auction it off with the proceeds to benefit the family for years to come? Unfortunately, Dr. King did not have a will to specify, but after reading this book, you will take such items into consideration when drafting a will.

In addition, a pastor should consider addressing the following:
- Intellectual property: published books, sermon notes, audio/visuals of sermons
- Clergy attire: robes, clergy shirts, capes, rings, crosses, bibles, crozier
  - Question: Do these items belong to the family, the church, or the denomination?

- Library: books, music and video collections, photos, trophies and awards, licenses, certificates, and degrees, etc.
- Collection Items – sports equipment or memorabilia, pets, including horses, guns, jewelry, souvenirs, etc.

The following are transcripts of two video blogs by the Law Office of Travell Travis, PLC, on the issue of having a will and keeping the will current.

LEGAL LESSON 11: FIRST PRINCE, NOW ARETHA: FIVE REASONS YOU MAY NOT NEED A WILL (AUGUST 24, 2018)

"As you know, it was reported yesterday that she [Aretha Franklin] passed away without a will or a trust. Today, I want to give you five (5) reasons why you may not need a will.

A will is a legal document that allows a person to decide who gets that individual's property when that individual dies. Without it, the state decides who gets what.

On the other hand, with a trust, someone is placed in charge of money or property for the benefit of someone else. For example, a grandmother leaves $100,000 for grandkids college education. This pot of money would be managed by a trustee for the grandchildren as they need money for college expenses such as tuition, room and board, supplies, travel, etc.

In the case of Aretha Franklin, her primary property would be her intellectual property. She owns most of the rights and royalties off her songs from her forty-plus albums and songs that she wrote for other performers. Copyrights last for life plus 70 years. Thus, for the next 70 years, her family will control and reap the financial benefits from that music. With a trust, she could have designated someone, a specific family member or a legal representative with understanding of the industry, to manage that catalog of music, rights and royalties, for the benefit of the children and grandchildren.

153

As it stands now, her four children share in ownership, control and financial benefit from that copyright. This arrangement may be fine for now but can potentially get more complex as her children pass away and the copyright interest is passed down, owned, and shared by the grandchildren and great-grandchildren. It will be no different than a family home that gets passed down from one generation to the next but runs the risk of losing the home because of failure to pay taxes or make necessary repairs.

Five reasons why a person may not need a will:

(1) The individual does not own any property.

Perhaps they rented their home, never owned a vehicle, lived paycheck-to-paycheck, and really do not have any property or assets worth passing down to anyone. Thus, why draft a will if the person does not own anything or have anything worth passing down to someone else? However, even this person may have clothes, jewelry, furniture, or family heirlooms; that might be valuable to someone else or point of contention amongst the heirs when they pass away. Grandma may have been poor and did not own a lot of nice things, but sometimes it is the few small things that can breed contention in a family. Families have been known to fight over photo albums, skillets, rocking chairs, blankets, and family bibles.

(2) The individual has already transferred all property to someone else.

Under this scenario, the individual has sold their home and furniture or transferred ownership of homes, vehicles, bank accounts, etc. to another family member. Alternatively, to perhaps downsize to live with another family member or reside in a retirement home or assisted living facility, they have literally given everything away already.

(3) The heir, who would inherit by will, would also inherit by intestate succession.

This is a possible reason not to draft a will when an individual desires for everything to go to their one and only spouse, child, sibling, or parent. Under this scenario it is still beneficial to have a will to expedite any transfer of property or to name an alternate beneficiary under a will. What happens if the assumed heir passes away, first, then what? With a will, a person could name an alternative individual or even a charity. Also, with a will, a person could create a trust to establish parameters for how the individual or alternative individual could receive or use the assets inherited.

I recall a client who was divorced and only had one child. Both of her parents were deceased. Yet, because the doctors had informed her that she only had a short time to live, she wanted to make sure all of her affairs (will, power of attorney, living will, etc.) were in order.[45] She did not want there to be any issues, complications, or delays, when it came to her daughter being able to handle her business.

(4) The individual really does not care or is undecided about who will get everything when they die.

As stated earlier, without a will, the government decides who inherits and then it's up to the heirs to decide amongst themselves; if there are more than one heir, who will actually get, whatever, or decide what to do with it. Sadly, especially in the black community, much wealth has been lost because family homes have been passed down to children, collectively, and because the siblings cannot agree on a plan for the property (e.g. sell it, rent it or give it away, etc.) or agree upon tax payments, the property ends up being taking by the government for the unpaid taxes. The property is then resold at auction to cover the unpaid taxes. The new owner is able to renovate and "flip" the house, especially in a gentrified neighborhood, making in some cases hundreds of thousands of dollars off of the property in a resale. Wealth lost and squandered because a plan was not in place for the property!

On the other hand, for those who are simply unsure, they should be reminded, a will can remain confidential (not its existence, but its

---

[45] It's not easy to receive a phone call from a family member or respected church leader stating they need a will ASAP because the doctors have just given them less than three months to live. It takes a measure of God's grace to separate one's personal feelings from one's professional responsibility in such cases. I vividly recall how we had prayer for her along with her daughter and two best friends that served as witnesses for her will. Thankfully, by the grace of God she lived an additional two years.

155

content) until death. Secondly, a will can be revised, amended, or revoked at any time prior to death or mental incapacity of the testator. Thus, if someone is uncomfortable with doing a last will and testament, as if it is written in stone like the ten commandments, understand it can be changed or held in confidence until the necessary time.

(5) The individual plans to live forever, never die, or be amongst the "alive and remain" when the rapture takes place.

This final point is more for satire, sarcasm, and cynicism rather than actual seriousness. However, even if people do believe this, that they will live forever, then surely, they live their lives, and handle their business, in this manner. This belief may be acceptable or tolerable for the lay members in your congregation. However, it is absolutely hypocritical to warn people to prepare for the inevitability of death from a spiritual standpoint, but not prepare for the inevitability of death from a temporal standpoint. Preparation for death, both from a spiritual and temporal standpoint, should not be viewed as mutually exclusive but should be planned in tandem.

LEGAL LESSON 14: THE JOHN SINGLETON DILEMMA – THE OUTDATED WILL (JUNE 19, 2019)

Recently, John Singleton, a well-known actor and comedian, passed away. His net worth is estimated to be $35 million. We also learned that he drafted a will back in 1993, leaving everything to his only child, at the time. The problem is that he had six (6) more kids, but never updated his will to include (or expressly exclude) any of them. Now his family is in court fighting over his estate.

Thus, the legal question: "Can I change my will?"

The short answer to this question is yes! A will does not become final until death and can be changed as long as the person is alive and has sufficient mental capacity. A will can be updated 1 of 2 ways: either by revocation or amendment. A revocation allows the person to cancel a previous will and essentially start over with a new will.

On the other hand, an amendment or codicil allows one to keep the original will but make changes or additions to the will. A codicil is best when the basic framework of the will is good, but perhaps assets or heirs need to be updated. A revocation and new will is probably best where the whole structure or framework of the will needs to be revamped due to substantial changes in family, assets, or desired distribution framework.

Ideally, one should review and revise their will annually – perhaps at a birthday, wedding anniversary, or as part of a new-year financial check-up.

Four key events to trigger a will review or revision:

1) Change in Family: births, adoptions, marriages, divorces (including the testator or one of the planned heirs), remarriages, or deaths. A will may need to be revoked or revised once a new generation is born (i.e. grandchildren or great-grandchildren) or an entire generation passes away (i.e. parents or grandparents). Wills are even more important today with the increasing number of blended families.

157

An individual could marry someone who has a child from a previous relationship, raise that child from infancy as if it were their own, but never formally adopt that child. A blood child could not have a closer bond, but legally, without adoption, they are not your child. The only way they can be treated as a child or heir is by adoption or by including them in a will as an heir.

Consequently, in the alternative, the individual has a blood child that they absolutely have no relationship with whatsoever. This child may be entitled to inherit something from their biological parent; absent a will that expressly excludes them from it.

Likewise, as family dynamics and relationships constantly change, a will may require updating to reflect the current status of those relationships. Duly noted, in the case where one has minor children, the only legal way to express who you may want to raise them in the case of your premature death is through a will. Having a christening and naming Godparents is good, but the official, legal, way to express your desire is in a will.

2) Change in Finances: promotions and pay raises, graduations, job changes, retirements, bankruptcies, won or lost lawsuits or judgments, new businesses, royalties, etc. In other words, a person's income, wealth, or financial status can change over a lifetime. This can have an impact or one's estate plan.

For example, a pastor who drafted their first will while in their 30's as a struggling, no-name, bi-vocational, store-front preacher; may be a multimillionaire, mega church pastor when they pass away. This person over the next 30 years now has best-selling books, international television ministry, portfolio of real estate holdings, and business interest in multiple companies by the time they reach the age of 60.

Is the original will sufficient? Maybe or maybe not! If under the original will everything went to the spouse and then to children equally, the framework may still work even if the amount of assets channeled through the funnel is larger than originally contemplated. If on the other hand, this individual wants to create a trust or have different things to go to different people, then a new will must be drafted.

3) Change in Assets & Property: anytime a person buys a home, real estate, automobiles, investments, inherited property or money, boats, rental property, stocks, collector's items, or business interest, should trigger a will review.

4) Change in Health: older, milestone birthdays, surgery, hospital stays, life-expectancy, family history, disability, accident or injury, diagnosed with a chronic or terminal illness, memory-loss conditions such as dementia or Alzheimer's disease, or a pandemic such as Covid-19 where anyone could potentially catch a fatal virus; should trigger a will review.

Prayerfully, none of these things will cause one's immediate death or demise, but should be considered as "triggers" to remind an individual that they are not here to stay and that now is a good time to review their estate plan.

In conclusion, this is not a complete list of things that should prompt a will review but should give an individual an idea of events that should trigger a review. First, have a will or estate plan. Second, make sure the will is up to date and reflects present finances and family relationships. Third, review and revise the will if there are changes in family, finances, property, or health. Lastly, make sure that the right person(s) knows that you have a will (and the latest version of that will), the general scheme of the estate place, where the will is located, and have access to it upon your death.

TRUSTS

As mentioned earlier, simply stated, a trust is a mechanism where the creator (settlor) sets aside money or property to be managed by a third party (trustee) for the benefit of someone else (beneficiary). A trust can be established while the settlor is alive (living or inter vivos trust) or established upon the settlor's death through a will (testamentary trust). A trust can be unchangeable or permanent (irrevocable trust) or amendable (revocable). A trust can be established for an individual, a group, or for a non-profit organization (charitable trust). The primary advantages of establishing a trust are the possible tax benefits and the ability to establish criteria as to how, or when, the funds from the trust can be used by the beneficiaries.

For example, an individual may own several rental properties. The owner may be concerned that beneficiaries do not, or cannot, manage the properties themselves. With a trust, a trustee could manage the rental properties for the benefit of the beneficiaries. The trust could establish that the income from the rental units or the profits from the sale of the properties go directly to beneficiaries as their primary or supplemental income.

Alternatively, the funds could be placed in a savings account to pay for a grandchild's future college education, long term care for a surviving spouse, down payment for a home, funds to start a business, donation to a church or college, or as a lump sum inheritance to a beneficiary once they reach a certain age (i.e. age 21) or milestone (i.e. graduate college). Moreover, the trust could provide for the selling of the rental property or asset or prohibit (with exceptions) the trust from selling the property or asset. Under this framework, the property or asset is deemed "untouchable." However, the beneficiaries could receive periodic payout from the income generated or interest accumulated. This is often the case where an individual has money, property or assets that can generate its own income. The beneficiary could simply "live off of" the accumulated interest, royalties, dividends, or capital gains without ever touching the actual property placed in the trust.

Thus, if an individual is interested in establishing a framework where their family members, or even their church, can benefit long term from one's assets, yet can control the parameters for how it can be spent, or to avoid certain tax consequences, then a trust may be a good route to pursue. Due to the possible complexity and implications of establishing a trust, it is highly recommended that an individual contact an attorney that specializes in trust or estate planning to create it.

PRENUPTIAL AGREEMENTS

Prenuptial agreements are often frowned upon in the church because it is assumed to mean an individual is contemplating divorce before getting married. However, while in some ways this may be true, it is not the only reason why a person may get a prenuptial agreement.

Most couples will accumulate wealth and assets together over the course of the marriage. However, with people getting married later in life - they may already own a home, business, or other property, prior to getting married. An individual may have already inherited money or assets from a family or will likely do so in the future. Under a prenuptial agreement, one can decide in advance to what extent will individual property become marital property.

This is even more so important with a second or subsequent marriages where children from a previous marriage are involved. A prenuptial may essentially say "if this marriage doesn't work, then what's mine stays mine, and what's your stays yours!" It also might address questions surrounding insurance or retirement benefits where a subsequent marriage might terminate those benefits from a previous marriage.

For example,   a widow receives a pension from her first husband so long as she remains unmarried. If she gets married, she could become the beneficiary under her new husband's retirement plan. But what happens if the second marriage fails and they end up getting a divorce. A prenuptial might state that the widow remains a beneficiary of her second husband's retirement plan.[46] A prenuptial could be signed to communicate to skeptical family members that the person is not getting married for their family member's money; whatever they have will remain in the family and go to

---

[46] The complexity of financial matters with seniors who desire to remarry often leads to many either opting for cohabiting unmarried or not getting married at all.

their children, not the new spouse or their children. Thus, even if a person does not get a prenuptial agreement for a first marriage, it may be beneficial to get one for a second marriage. This is not because you anticipate divorce, but to ensure that your children get your property when you pass, not your new spouse or their children.

A GOOD NAME

"A good name is rather to be chosen than great riches, and loving favour rather than silver and gold"(Proverbs 22:1 KJV).

"And David said, is there yet any that is left of the house of Saul, that I may shew him kindness for Jonathan's sake? And there was of the house of Saul a servant whose name was Ziba. And when they had called him unto David, the king said unto him, Art thou Ziba? And he said, thy servant is he. And the king said, is there not yet any of the house of Saul, that I may shew the kindness of God unto him? And Ziba said unto the king, Jonathan hath yet a son, which is lame on his feet. And the king said unto him, where is he? And Ziba said unto the king, Behold, he is in the house of Machir, the son of Ammiel, in Lodebar.

Then king David sent, and fetched him out of the house of Machir, the son of Ammiel, from Lodebar. Now when Mephibosheth, the son of Jonathan, the son of Saul, was come unto David, he fell on his face, and did reverence. And David said, Mephibosheth. And he answered, Behold thy servant! And David said unto him, Fear not: for I will surely shew thee kindness for Jonathan thy father's sake and will restore thee all the land of Saul thy father; and thou shalt eat bread at my table continually. And he bowed himself, and said, what is thy servant, that thou shouldest look upon such a dead dog as I am?

Then the king called to Ziba, Saul's servant, and said unto him, I have given unto thy master's son all that pertained to Saul and to all his house. Thou therefore, and thy sons, and thy servants, shall till the land for him, and thou shalt bring in the fruits, that thy master's son may have food to eat: but Mephibosheth thy master's son shall eat bread always at my table. Now Ziba had fifteen sons and twenty servants.

Then said Ziba unto the king, according to all that my lord the king hath commanded his servant, so shall thy servant do. As for Mephibosheth, said the king, he shall eat at my table, as one of the king's sons. And Mephibosheth had a young son, whose name was Micha. And all that dwelt in the house of Ziba were servants unto Mephibosheth. So, Mephibosheth dwelt in Jerusalem: for he did eat continually at the king's table; and was lame on both his feet" (II Samuel 9:1-13 KJV).

Jonathan did not have an inheritance, but because of his good name and loyalty to David, his son Mephibosheth received Saul's inheritance! A man or woman of God, who has been faithful to God and in serving God's people, may not have many earthly possessions to pass down to their children when they die. However, just as David blessed the heir of Jonathan, God has a way of blessing one's children and grandchildren. Never forget that one of the greatest things you can pass down to your children is a great name! Not in the sense of celebrity or notoriety, but to be known as a family of faith, people of God, prayer and praise, with character, morals, and values.

The bible remembers Enoch as one who "walked with God" (Genesis 5:24); Noah as a "preacher of righteousness" (Peter 2:25); Abraham was a "friend of God" (James 2:23); Moses was "very meek, above all the men which were upon the face of the earth" (Numbers 12:3); Job as a man that was "perfect and upright, and one that feared God, and eschewed evil" (Job 1:1); and David was "a man after mine own heart, which shall fulfill all my will" (Acts 13:22). To God be the glory for the inheritance you might leave behind, but what will be your legacy? What your family and congregation will be able to say about your life and legacy will matter the most!

"Just let me live my life,
Let it be pleasing, Lord to Thee,

out and if I gain any praise,
Let it go to Calvary.
To God be the glory
For the things He has done."

CHAPTER 12
ALIVE BUT UNABLE TO PERFORM –
PREPARING FOR THE POSSIBILITY OF DISABILITY

Picture this: a middle-aged pastor of a thriving church has a massive stroke only a few years after moving into a newly built state of the art facility. For a while, no one knew whether the pastor would even survive the stroke. Yet a few weeks later he is stable, regains consciousness, and is released to a rehabilitation center. A few months later, after intensive rehab, he regained his mobility to walk and care for himself. However, a year has gone by, and there is one aspect of his life that he has not regained – his ability to speak!

What is a pastor or church supposed to do under these circumstances? Who is in charge the first Sunday after the pastor has the stroke? Who is in charge while the pastor is in the rehabilitation center? What should a church do when it is clear that unless God intervenes with a miracle; the pastor is unlikely to recover his ability to speak again? How long will the congregation stay together not knowing if their pastor will resume his duties? Can the pastor be forced into retirement? Who makes that decision? Can the church afford to financially support their former pastor and a new pastor at the same time? Can the church continue to maintain mortgage payments if donations are down during this period of uncertainty? Does the pastor's spouse have any say or protection in the matter? At this point, the church has moved beyond the question as to whether the pastor will survive the stroke. The question now is whether the church will survive the pastor having the stroke!

Unfortunately, this story is too familiar and too common. Even if it is not a stroke, perhaps it's a heart attack, cancer diagnosis, dementia or

Alzheimer's disease.   Is there a plan for temporary or emergency leadership?   Is there a documented process in place for making a permanent change in leadership when the pastor is still alive?   Not to diminish the complexity of replacing a deceased pastor, however, it is more complex when the pastor is alive, yet no longer able to serve.

Every case and situation is different.   One person can have a stroke, remain wheelchair bound for the rest of their life, but have their full mind, ability to speak, and can continue to serve as pastor. Someone with cancer can undergo treatments on Mondays and be back in the pulpit by the following Sunday. On the other hand, someone may have major heart surgery and be out of the pulpit for the next 3 to 6 months. Then what is a congregation to do?

Even if plans are in place for someone who is middle-aged or older, do you have plans in place for a perfectly healthy individual that could end up in the hospital due to a car accident or some other unfortunate injury? God forbid another pandemic like Covid-19 hits the globe again, what is the plan? Under what circumstances, should a pastor's position be impacted by a short-term, long-term, or permanent disability? Can the person still function, or has it severely impaired their ability to serve effectively as the pastor?

HEALTH AND DISABILITY INSURANCE

A bivocational pastor often remains on their secular job, not just for the income, but for the benefits. Statistics indicate that a worker has a 30% chance of getting disabled. Twelve percent of the population receive disability benefits and another 12 percent will be on disability for a period of five years or less during their working years.[47] Does the pastor's compensation package provide for paid sick-leave, health insurance, short-term/long-term disability insurance, or long term care insurance?

Even if one is able to accept a lower salary as a full time pastor, can you afford to move to full- time ministry if your church cannot provide

---

[47] www.disabilitylawyer.com retrieved June 17, 2020.

you with a comparable benefits package? Will the spouse be able to provide health and disability benefits through their secular job? Does the church denomination provide health, disability, and retirement benefits for its pastors? No one wants to see their pastor in a nursing home, but can a church afford to provide an in-home nurse or to put them in a top-tier assisted living facility? These questions, and more, should be taken into consideration when putting together a pastor's compensation package and succession plan.

Health Insurance: If not provided through church, spouse, denomination, or secular employment, a pastor should consider obtaining a private plan, a plan through the Affordable Care Act (Obama Care), or consider applying for Medicaid or investing in a health savings account. Hospitals cost on average $3,949 per day and each hospital stay costs an average of $15,734. A recent Kaiser study reported that 1 in 4 bankruptcies in America were due to the inability to pay a recent medical bill.[48]

Even with medical insurance, the copays and deductible for a simple trip to the emergency room can cost several thousands of dollars. For most Americans, this type of money isn't available in a savings account. Even if so, it will likely eliminate or severely diminish anyone's savings by having only one uninsured trip to the doctor.[49] As pastors, we have faith in God to protect and heal, but in America, you need health insurance, too!

Family Medical Leave Act (FMLA) requires certain employers to provide up to 12-weeks of medical sick leave during a 12-month time period. The 12 weeks may be used on a consecutive or intermittent basis.

[48] New Kaiser/New York Times Survey Finds One in Five Working-Age Americans With Health Insurance Report Problems Paying Medical Bills Published: Jan 05, 2016 https://www.kff.org/health-costs/report/the-burden-of-medical-debt-results-from-the-kaiser-family-foundationnew-york-times-medical-bills-survey/ retrieved June 17, 2020.

[49] Many churches and ministries have started paying off medical debt for families in the community to help them avoid foreclosure and bankruptcy. In 2019, Mark Moore, Jr. and Young Leader's Conference (YLC) received national attention for paying off over $1 million dollars in medical debt for families in Atlanta who were on the verge of bankruptcy. https://www.prnewswire.com/news-releases/young-leaders-conference-ylc-pays-off-1-5-million-dollars-in-medical-debt-for-over-1--200-underserved-families-in-atlanta-area-300905213.html retrieved June 17, 2020.

Generally speaking, during this time period, an employer must hold the position open for the employee to return. Often what is most misunderstood about FMLA is that the sick leave is unpaid! Hence, if a church falls under FMLA, and the pastor is a paid employee, but unable to perform pastoral duties for 12 weeks, the church may be required to retain their job, but will the church be able to continue to pay the pastor's salary during this period?

Even with a kind, benevolent, and compassionate church, it may be a financial strain to pay the pastor their full-time salary. A church might experience a decline in attendance or finances or may have to provide a stipend or love gift to guest speakers or to a substitute pastor during the interim period. One of the ways to alleviate this financial strain on the church is to provide the pastor with Short-Term Disability Insurance.

Short-Term Disability Insurance typically covers 40-60% of an employee's regular wages for 9-52 weeks depending on the policy. Coverage can commence immediately or a few weeks after the employee is unable to work. Injuries from accidents, surgeries, cancer, or even childbirth itself, may be covered under Short-Term Disability Insurance. Due to the fact that an individual may need short-term disability insurance during the course of their career, the premium may be slightly higher for short-term disability insurance than for long-term disability insurance. However,   it may be money well spent when one is out of work for medical reasons and still needs money to cover their bills.

Long-Term Disability Insurance typically covers 50-70% of an employee's regular wages for 5-10 years, or as long as the employee is disabled, up until the age of 65. At age 65, Medicare and Social Security is likely to provide income and medical coverage to the individual. Coverage under long-term disability insurance usually commences 10-53 weeks after the employee is unable to work. Long-Term Disability Insurance may cover more severe, long-term, chronic, or terminal medical matters or permanent disability (i.e. cancer, cardiovascular, musculoskeletal, back disorders, nervous system, severe injuries, cancer, etc.) therefore coverage usually begin after the time period that short-term disability ends.

Long-Term Care Insurance: What happens when the pastor is unable to care for themselves at home but is unable to provide in-home care or afford a top-tier retirement facility? One of the options is to purchase Long-Term Care Insurance. Long-Term Care Insurance can cover the cost of in-home care, assisted living, adult daycare, nursing home, and home modification. Long-term Care Insurance may also pay for a 24/7 live-in caregiver, companion, housekeeper, therapist or a private-duty nurse. With a Long-Term Care Insurance policy, the individual, family, and church may have more resources to provide for the long-term care of the pastor. Long-Term Care Insurance may also provide tax benefits, a death benefit, and often can be purchased along with a life insurance policy.

POWER OF ATTORNEY

A power of attorney gives another person the legal authority to transact business on one's behalf in case of mental or physical incapacity. In general, there are two types of powers of attorney: springing and durable. Springing allows an individual to set up the power of attorney now but have a predetermined triggering event in the future for when it would become effective. A durable power of attorney means that even when a person is not capacitated, the power of attorney is still effective.

One can craft a very broad or very narrow power of attorney. Meaning, an individual can decide what business matters are, or are not, covered. One could also include multiple people either as co-powers, alternate-powers, or substitute powers. While most typically think of powers-of-attorney when someone is mentally or physically incapacitated, there may be other reason why someone might create one.

For example, athletes and entertainers often give their agents, managers, or trusted family members power of attorney because they are so busy with their careers that they do not have time to manage their personal affairs. Likewise, someone who may be going away for an extended period of time, such as a soldier in the military or even a convicted individual going to jail, might craft at least a temporary power-of-attorney so that someone can manage their business affairs while they are away. Similarly, an itinerant minister, an international evangelist, or foreign missionary, who might be out of the country for an extended period of time, might all benefit from having a power of attorney.

The key to having a power of attorney is being able to trust the person who you give the authority and have confidence that they will make wise and prudent business decisions. Many have heard how trusted individuals have made poor investments, squandered large sums of money, or out-right "robbed" the person they were obligated to serve. In one instance, a child used his mother's social security check to buy drugs, leaving his mother without food and utilities. Another instance, a grandchild forced their grandparent into a nursing home by selling their house while they were away in rehab. So be careful! Yet without a power-of-attorney, one might still lose everything if someone is not empowered to manage an individual's business affairs when they are disabled or incapacitated.

Further noted, designating someone as an executor of a will or as an administrator of an estate is not the same as designating someone as a power-of-attorney. Typically, a power of attorney commences when stated and ends upon the death of the individual. On the other hand, an administrator or executive starts at the time of one's death and lasts until they have wrapped up the affairs of the deceased. Thus, a single individual can be designated to handle both: pre-death matters and post-death matters. The former must be established in a power-of-attorney, whereas the later must be established by will or state law.

LIVING WILLS

A living will is an instrument that places in writing one's desires regarding end of life decisions. Do you know under what conditions you would want to fight to live or be allowed to die? Do you want to stay alive if it requires artificial means to sustain you? Are you willing to be placed on a feeding tube, ventilator, or a cardiopulmonary bypass machine? Do not resuscitate for a simple choking or kept on life support when a person is clearly brain dead? Do you want your family to exhaust every option to keep you alive or do you want them to end your suffering as soon as possible?

Is there someone who cares enough about you, but also is emotionally stable, rational, and capable of understanding medical options, that can make the best decision for you? During the 1990's, there was a young lady, Terry Schiavo, who was essentially brain dead. Her parents wanted to keep her alive. However, her husband wanted to remove her feeding tube so she could stop suffering and die peacefully. After numerous court cases and debates in Congress, it was affirmed that without a living will, it was ultimately up to the next of kin, to make end of life decisions. In Schiavo's case, it was her husband, and not her parents, who would make that final decision.

For some, having a spouse make the final decision may not be in their best interest, especially, if they are glad to see you go! On the other hand, they may want to keep you around as long as possible even if it means keeping you alive in a vegetative state. Having a living will not only predetermine the conditions by which one is sustained, but also predetermines who will make the final call.

Is there a biblical principle to guide someone in this decision? During the bible days, they did not have life sustaining technology. On one hand, God is a healer, miracle worker, and has the final say over life and death. In fact, God can raise a man from the dead! On the other hand, is it okay for someone to end their life when they know they are about to die or have absolutely zero chance of recovering? When Saul was mortally wounded in battle, did he commit suicide or expedite the inevitable? Let's examine the Scripture.

"The Philistines fought against Israel, and the Israelites ran away from them. Many Israelites were killed at Mount Gilboa. The Philistines fought hard against Saul and his sons. They killed his sons Jonathan, Abinadab and Malki-Shua. The fighting became bad around Saul. When the archers shot at him, he was badly wounded. He said to the officer who

171

carried his armor, "Pull out your sword and kill me. Then those uncircumcised men won't make fun of me and kill me." But Saul's officer refused because he was afraid. So, Saul took his own sword and threw himself on it." (I Samuel 31:1-4 ICB - emphasis added).

HEALTH CARE DIRECTIVES

Akin to a Living Wills, a health care directive is a written instrument that designates someone to make healthcare decisions for someone else. The primary difference between a living will and a health care directive is that the living will is specific to end-of-life decisions whereas a Health Care Directive allows someone to make all types of medical decisions when one is unable to make them for themselves.

For example, someone may be in a coma after a car accident. The injuries from the accident are not deemed to be live threatening. However, the individual is unconscious, unable to speak, and may have a long road to recovery. However, at the moment, someone has to make urgent critical decisions regarding their immediate care. Once again, without a health care directive, the decision would be in the hands of the next of kin: if married, spouse; or if unmarried, parents, children, or siblings. This may also all depend on the age of the individual or the age of the children. If parents and spouse are deceased, then it would likely fall on the adult children by committee[50]. Depending on family size and dynamics, you can imagine how complicated it might be to make these types of decisions by committee. One may opt to place the decision in the hands of a specific family member or someone who otherwise would not be in the "chain of command" such as a sibling, best friend, or significant other.

---

[50] I recall early in my career where a mother had a severe stroke. Her older children that lived out of town did not want to see their mother suffer any longer and wished to "pull the plug." The youngest child, who lived with her mother, said "not yet, I still have hope that she will recover!" Thankfully, she was able to convince her siblings to hold off a while longer. A few weeks later their mother was at home from the hospital, fully recovered!

CHAPTER 13
WHEN TO HANG-UP THE CLEATS:
PREPARING FOR RETIREMENT

"I BROUGHT GLORY TO YOU HERE ON EARTH BY COMPLETING THE WORK YOU GAVE ME TO DO." ~ JESUS[51]

A PROPHET FORCED TO RETIRE

"When Samuel grew old, he appointed his sons as judges over Israel. His firstborn son's name was Joel and his second was Abijah. They were judges in Beer-sheba. However, his sons did not walk in his ways—they turned toward dishonest gain, took bribes, and perverted justice. So, all the elders of Israel gathered together and went to Samuel at Ramah. They said to him, "Look, you are old, and your sons do not follow your example. Therefore, appoint a king to judge us the same as all the other nations have."

When they said, "Give us a king to judge us," Samuel considered their demand sinful, so he prayed to the LORD. But the LORD told him, "Listen to the people and everything they say to you. They have not rejected you; they have rejected Me as their king. They are doing the same thing to you that they have done to Me, since the day I brought them out of Egypt until this day, abandoning Me and worshiping other gods. Listen to them, but you must solemnly warn them and tell them about the rights of the king who will rule over them" (I Samuel 8:1-8 ICB).

This passage is not used to suggest that asking a leader to retire is tantamount to rejecting God or making a sinful demand. However, the

---

[51] John 17:4 NLT

feeling of rejection by Samuel is relatable to any leader being asked or forced to retire. Further, it may be in the divine will of God for a change of leadership at the time. While Saul in many ways would end up being a failure as king, God's hand was definitely on David, Solomon, and many other future kings of Israel.

Moreover, what is probably the most important and applicable lesson from Samuel's retirement is how Samuel continued to serve God and the nation after his tenure as the nation's judge came to an end. When Samuel retired as a judge for Israel, he did not give up his role as a priest or as a prophet in Israel. (See I Samuel 13:8-16). In addition, God called upon Samuel to anoint two different kings for Israel. Upon further examination of Samuel's retirement, the only thing that changed was Samuel's daily duties of judging the people and fighting in wars with the Philistines.

For the remainder of Samuel's life--some would say even after his death-- Samuel remained in an oversight position in Israel. Samuel would provide Saul with both spiritual and military guidance. In many ways, Samuel was Saul's pastor. Samuel would live several years after transferring his role as leader of Israel over to Saul and remained influential in the kingdom until his death. Samuel would also spend the remainder of his years serving as "dean" or "principal" of the school of prophets.

Biblically speaking, even the Levites were required to retire from their daily duties at age fifty (See Numbers 8:23-26). This retirement was not a complete cessation of work but a shifting of job duties more appropriate for their physical abilities and experience. Specifically, the retired Levites no longer had to participate in the heavy lifting and transporting of the tabernacle, its furniture, instruments, and the various offerings and sacrifices. Similarly, with dimming vision, the older priests no longer had the sole responsibility for diagnosing and inspecting individuals suspected of having leprosy.

However, the retired Levites could attend and assist their brethren with the performance of their duties in the tabernacle. In the New

Testament, we read of Zacharias (father of John the Baptist), "well stricken in years" yet "executed the priest's office before God" and "his lot was to burn incense when he went into the temple of the Lord" (Luke 1:7-8 KJV). Moreover, the retired Levites were permitted to continue to "earn a salary" from the congregation for the remainder of their lives (Numbers 18:1-32; Deuteronomy 18:1-8 KJV). Thus, for a Levite, retirement did not equate to becoming obsolete or non-essential, but a repositioning of the individual to a role where they could be more useful and effective.

Several things could impact one's decision on if, or when, to retire. A leader's age, health, fatigue-level, biblical view, God's leading and the current condition of the ministry must be taken into consideration. Hopefully, it is not merely the lack of finances or the failure to groom a successor that caused one to refuse to retire. A church might not have invested in a retirement savings account in the past or be able to afford multiple salaries in the present.

One might in fact pastor until death, but it is great to at least have the option to retire. If prepared in advance, a former pastor could retire, but remain a paid member of staff with the title or designation as founding or senior pastor, pastor emeritus, bishop of the house, apostle, or chairman of the board. With this new title and job description the former pastor could be free to become a church planter, foreign missionary, church consultant, or establish a "school of the prophets" for aspiring pastors and ministers. The key is knowing the will of God, proper planning, and doing what is best for yourself and your congregation. The choice is yours. Do you want to "walk off the field" on your own terms or be "carted off the field" (literally by way of a casket) when you end your tenure as pastor?

On a side note, the decision to retire as a local pastor may be necessary if a leader is elevated to an office such as diocese/jurisdiction bishop or presiding bishop of a denomination. Such positions often require extensive travel and time away from a local church in order to be effective. It may be important for such leaders to retain a "home church" and have opportunities to minister, participate in counseling parishioners, be involved

175

in decision making, and oversee the transition in leadership or succession plan implemented.

All this can be arranged to avoid the stress and responsibility that comes with being 24-7, on-demand, full-time pastor. In many cases, the decision to retire has little to do with the present leader's health, vision, or capacity to lead. In fact, it may be because God has called the leader to a higher position in the Kingdom. Why limit yourself to one church when there may be hundreds of pastors and churches that need you! Indeed, a preacher can never stop preaching, but God may release you from pastoring.

OPTING OUT OF SOCIAL SECURITY

One of the most commonly misunderstood options reserved for clergy is the ability to opt out of paying into social security. Numerous online articles, books, and financial conferences present the option as merely a tax exemption for clergy members. However, opting out of social security is not merely a tax exemption for clergy but a rejection to the entire system based on religious beliefs. Thus, to opt out of social security, a minister must swear under oath that for religious reasons one does not believe in social security or financial support from the government. By making such a declaration, a minister is not merely exempt from social security taxes but is also exempted from receiving other government benefits such as: Medicare, disability payments, death payments to minor kids or widows, and a social security check when retired. Below is the declaration a minister must make under oath in order to be exempt from paying social security taxes. It is fair to say that many, if not most, are not opposed to government aid or support because of their religious beliefs.

I certify that I am conscientiously opposed to, or because of my religious principles I am opposed to, the acceptance (for services I perform as a minister, member of a religious order not under a vow of poverty, or Christian Science practitioner) of any public insurance that makes payments in the event of death, disability, old age, or retirement; or that

176

makes payments toward the cost of, or provides services for, medical care. (Public insurance includes insurance systems established by the Social Security Act.)

I certify that as a duly ordained, commissioned, or licensed minister of a church or a member of a religious order not under a vow of poverty, I have informed the ordaining, commissioning, or licensing body of my church or order that I am conscientiously opposed to, or because of religious principles I am opposed to, the acceptance (for services I perform as a minister or as a member of a religious order) of any public insurance that makes payments in the event of death, disability, old age, or retirement; or that makes payments toward the cost of, or provides services for, medical care, including the benefits of any insurance system established by the Social Security Act.

I certify that I have never filed Form 2031 to revoke a previous exemption from social security coverage on earnings as a minister, member of a religious order not under a vow of poverty, or Christian Science practitioner. I request to be exempted from paying self-employment tax on my earnings from services as a minister, member of a religious order not under a vow of poverty, or Christian Science practitioner, under section 1402(e) of the Internal Revenue Code. I understand that the exemption, if granted, will apply only to these earnings. Under penalties of perjury, I declare that I have examined this application and to the best of my knowledge and belief, it is true and correct.

IF one opts out of social security, the money saved should not be viewed as extra spending money. The extra money should be used to save or invest elsewhere for healthcare and retirement. A minister can place the funds in other investment options to help them save and even grow their retirement funds. Such investment options include, but are not limited to real estate, money market accounts, certificates of deposit, stock market, or some other private retirement plans IRA's, 401(k)'s, and annuities.

If a minister is bi-vocational, they may opt to invest in their employer-sponsored retirement or pension plan, especially if the employer has a matching policy. Word of caution, if you opt out of social security to self-handle your retirement and health care, make sure you do not mishandle it! If you do, it will be up to you and God to take care of you for the remainder of your life!

IS 40 YEARS LONG ENOUGH?

Headline: March 2020, Bill Gates, forty-four years after founding Microsoft, withdraws from Microsoft board to become a full-time philanthropist. Bill Gates co-founded Microsoft with Paul Allen in 1975. Gates served as CEO until 2000, and then as a full-time executive until 2008. In 2014, he stepped down from the role of executive chairman. His last position included technical advisor and general board member. Upon retirement, Gates will only retain the position of technical advisor, by request of the current CEO, Satya Nadella.

After his retirement Gates is quoted as saying he is "more optimistic than ever about the progress the company is making and how it can continue to benefit the world." Gates, 70, stated he wants "to dedicate more time to philanthropic priorities including global health and development, education, and my increasing engagement in tackling climate change." At the time of Gate's retirement, Microsoft is now a trillion-dollar company, reaching a value that it never approached while he served as CEO. Gates retires retaining 1.3% of the company's shares – a present value of approximately $16 billion.[52]

Biblically speaking, does forty years of service have any significance? The Bible does not give specifics about pastoring, but it does give several examples for the tenure of Israel's leaders. Generally, all monarchs served until their death. The range is from Zimri's tenure of only one week (I Kings 16:15) to Uzziah and Manasseh's tenures surpassing over five decades. Notable leaders of Israel that served forty or more years

---

[52] Bill Gates leaves Microsoft board, PUBLISHED FRI, MAR 13 20205:09 PM EDT, https://www.cnbc.com/2020/03/13/bill-gates-leaves-microsoft-board.html, Retrieved June 15, 2020.

include: Moses (40 years - Acts 7:23, 30) Saul (40 years - Acts 12:21), David (40 years - I Kings 2:11), Solomon (40 years - I Kings 11:42) Asa (41 years - II Chronicles 16:13), Joash (40 years - II Chronicles 24:1), Uzziah (52 years - II Chronicles 26:3) and Manasseh (55 years – II Chronicles 33:1).

During their 40 years, most had tremendous success. However, sadly most who served 40 or more years, also saw things derail towards the end of their administration. Several kings were corrupt from the beginning, but many who served a long time started out with a heart towards God, unfortunately ended up with a heart turned away from God by the end of their tenure. The sole exception is Manasseh who became king at the age of 12, served 55 years, was initially known as Judah's most corrupt king, but at the end of his life, repented and turned his heart towards God. An examination of the other kings, paint a similar and sad end of their life and tenure as leaders[53]:

ASA

"So Abijah slept with his fathers, and they buried him in the city of David: and Asa his son reigned in his stead. In his days, the land was quiet ten years. And Asa did that which was good and right in the eyes of the LORD his God: For he took away the altars of the strange gods, and the high places, and brake down the images, and cut down the groves: And commanded Judah to seek the LORD God of their fathers, and to do the law and the commandment. Also, he took away out of all the cities of Judah the high places and the images: and the kingdom was quiet before him..."

"The things Asa did as king, from the beginning to the end, are written down. They are in the book of the kings of Judah and Israel. In the thirty-ninth year of his rule, Asa got a disease in his feet. His disease was very bad. But he did not ask for help from the Lord. He only asked for help from the doctors. Then Asa died in the forty-first year of his rule. The people buried Asa in the tomb he had made for himself in Jerusalem. They laid him

---

[53] Moses, David, and Solomon are discussed in other chapters in this book.

on a bed. It was filled with spices and different kinds of mixed perfumes. And they made a large fire to honor Asa" (II Chronicles 16:11-14 ICB).

JOASH

"Joash was seven years old when he became king. And he ruled 40 years in Jerusalem. His mother's name was Zibiah. She was from Beersheba. Joash did what the Lord said was right as long as Jehoiada the priest was alive"

Then the Spirit of God entered Zechariah son of Jehoiada the priest. Zechariah stood before the people and said, "This is what God says: 'Why do you disobey the Lord's commands? You will not be successful. You have left the Lord. So, the Lord has also left you.' "But the king and his officers made plans against Zechariah. The king commanded them to kill Zechariah. So, they threw stones at him in the Temple courtyard until he died. King Joash did not remember Jehoiada's kindness to him. So Joash killed Zechariah, Jehoiada's son. Before Zechariah died, he said, "May the Lord see what you are doing and punish you."

At the end of the year, the Aramean army came against Joash. They attacked Judah and Jerusalem and killed all the leaders of the people. Then they sent all the valuable things to their king in Damascus. The Aramean army came with only a small group of men. But the Lord let them defeat a very large army from Judah. He did this because the people of Judah had left the Lord. He is the God their ancestors followed. So Joash was punished. When the Arameans left, Joash was badly wounded. His own officers made plans against him. They did this because he had killed Zechariah son of Jehoiada the priest. So, they killed Joash in his own bed. He died and was buried in Jerusalem. But he was not buried in the graves of the kings" (II Chronicles 24:1-2, 20-26 KJV).

UZZIAH

"Sixteen years old was Uzziah when he began to reign, and he reigned fifty and two years in Jerusalem. His mother's name also was

Jecoliah of Jerusalem. And he did that which was right in the sight of the LORD, according to all that his father Amaziah did. And he sought God in the days of Zechariah, who had understanding in the visions of God: and as long as he sought the LORD, God made him to prosper..."

But when he was strong, his heart was lifted up to his destruction: for he transgressed against the LORD his God and went into the temple of the LORD to burn incense upon the altar of incense. And Azariah the priest went in after him, and with him fourscore priests of the LORD, that were valiant men: And they withstood Uzziah the king, and said unto him, It appertaineth not unto thee, Uzziah, to burn incense unto the LORD, but to the priests the sons of Aaron, that are consecrated to burn incense: go out of the sanctuary; for thou hast trespassed; neither shall it be for thine honour from the LORD God.

Then Uzziah was wroth, and had a censer in his hand to burn incense: and while he was wroth with the priests, the leprosy even rose up in his forehead before the priests in the house of the LORD, from beside the incense altar. And Azariah the chief priest, and all the priests, looked upon him, and, behold, he was leprous in his forehead, and they thrust him out from thence; yea, himself hasted also to go out, because the LORD had smitten him.

And Uzziah the king was a leper unto the day of his death, and dwelt in a several house, being a leper; for he was cut off from the house of the LORD: and Jotham his son was over the king's house, judging the people of the land. Now the rest of the acts of Uzziah, first and last, did Isaiah the prophet, the son of Amoz, write. So Uzziah slept with his fathers, and they buried him with his fathers in the field of the burial which belonged to the kings; for they said, He is a leper: and Jotham his son reigned in his stead" (II Chronicles 26:3-5; 16-22 KJV – emphasis added).

MANASSEH

"Manasseh was twelve years old when he began to reign, and he reigned fifty and five years in Jerusalem: But did that which was evil in the

181

sight of the LORD, like unto the abominations of the heathen, whom the LORD had cast out before the children of Israel..."

"Wherefore the LORD brought upon them the captains of the host of the king of Assyria, which took Manasseh among the thorns, and bound him with fetters, and carried him to Babylon. And when he was in affliction, he besought the LORD his God, and humbled himself greatly before the God of his fathers, And prayed unto him: and he was intreated of him, and heard his supplication, and brought him again to Jerusalem into his kingdom. Then Manasseh knew that the LORD he was God..."

"And he took away the strange gods, and the idol out of the house of the LORD, and all the altars that he had built in the mount of the house of the LORD, and in Jerusalem, and cast them out of the city. And he repaired the altar of the LORD, and sacrificed thereon peace offerings and thank offerings, and commanded Judah to serve the LORD God of Israel" (II Chronicles 33: 1-2, 11-13, 15-16 KJV).

If examined together, what is the common strain between all of these leaders? It is the spirit of pride! Pride caused Satan to believe he should be worshipped like God. If a leader is not careful, after decades of successful leadership, the one thing that can undermine their entire tenure is pride. Pride will cause a leader to lose focus, worship their accomplishments, and rely on self, more than God, for continued direction and success.

A leader has to consider whether remaining in office is motivated by pride or ego? Have you created an idol out of what you have built? The Scripture warns us "For what shall it profit a man, if he shall gain the whole world, and lose his own soul?" (Mark 8:36 KJV). If holding on to leadership will cause an individual to lose their soul, it's better to walk away early, rather than to stay too long, and go wrong!

THE GIFT OF RETIREMENT

"God wants everyone to eat and drink and be happy in his work. These are gifts from God" (Ecclesiastes 3:13 ICB).

"So, I saw the best thing a person can do is to enjoy his work. That is all he has. No one can help a person see what will happen in the future" (Ecclesiastes 3:22 ICB).

"God gives some people the ability to enjoy the wealth and property he gives them. He also gives them the ability to accept their state in life and enjoy their work" (Ecclesiastes 6:19 ICB).

In our secular professions we spend a lifetime working, preparing, and anticipating the day of retirement. Spiritually, we look forward to a day of rest for the saints of God. Hebrews declares *"There remaineth therefore a rest to the people of God. Let us labour therefore to enter into that rest, lest any man fall after the same example of unbelief"* (Hebrews 4:9, 11 KJV). If we can appreciate this concept both professionally and spiritually, one should also appreciate the same idea when it comes to pastoring. Don't view retirement as a rejection of your years of service, but a time of reaping after years of sowing!

CHAPTER 14
LIFE AFTER DEATH: LIFE INSURANCE AND FUNERAL ARRANGEMENTS

"Then Jehoshaphat rested with his ancestors and was buried with them in the City of David. And Jehoram his son succeeded him as king. Jehoram's brothers, the sons of Jehoshaphat, were Azariah, Jehiel, Zechariah, Azariahu, Michael and Shephatiah. All these were sons of Jehoshaphat king of Israel. Their father had given them many gifts of silver and gold and articles of value, as well as fortified cities in Judah, but he had given the kingdom to Jehoram because he was his firstborn son" (II Chronicles 21:1-3 NIV).

Some of you are reading and already thinking, "Well, I'm not a king; I can't be expected to leave my children cities or a huge fortune!" However, the bible declares that a good man will leave an inheritance, not just for his children, but enough to also benefit his grandchildren. Proverbs 13:22 (KJV) declares, "A good man leaveth an inheritance to his children's children: and the wealth of the sinner is laid up for the just." The Common English Bible makes the point even clearer when it states, "If you obey God, you will have something to leave your grandchildren. If you don't obey God, those who live right will get what you leave" (Proverbs 13:22 CEV). While it may be difficult to accumulate enough wealth in one's lifetime to leave a sizable inheritance to children, one of the easiest, and most affordable, ways to do so is by having a life insurance policy.

With a life insurance policy one can leave behind thousands, if not millions, of dollars to the next generation, tax free, for a nominal monthly fee. Yet sadly, according to a LIMRA report, "only fifty-night percent of Americans have life insurance, and about half of those with insurance are underinsured." Further compounded the problem is "close to 12 percent of whole life policies lapse in the first year and 10 percent lapse in the second year" with the rates being even higher for term life insurance. Taken together, these statistics prove that many are missing out on the opportunity to transfer wealth to the next generation through life insurance.

The cost for a life insurance policy will depend on one's age, health, life expectancy, type of policy (Term, Whole Life, Term, or Universal Life) and the desired coverage amount. A young man in his 20's might be able to find a million-dollar policy for less than $50 per month; whereas for $50 a month, a man in his 50's may only be able to get $250,000 in coverage. [54] The rates are even better for females.

Even if one has a current policy, the next question is whether the amount of the policy is sufficient to meet the financial goals of the individual. Is the policy merely to cover burial expenses, outstanding bills, or to pay off an existing car note or home mortgage? Alternatively, is the purpose for having the life insurance policy more lofty goals such as income replacement, charitable contribution, college funds, or wealth transfer to named beneficiaries?

Whether you or the church owns the insurance policy, a pastor should also consider such things as income for a living or surviving spouse. Can the church afford to pay your salary to your surviving spouse and to the new pastor at the same time, especially if the surviving spouse sacrificed and served along with you during your tenure? Have you considered how the church will pay off existing church debts, provide supplemental income for any dips or fluctuation in church income during the transition period, or to complete the vision to erect a new sanctuary or multi-purpose facility?

---

[54] **Life insurance statistics in 2020** https://www.policygenius.com/life-insurance/life-insurance-statistics/?fbclid=IwAR3tHE9b1VCUG-BWg4h2bGbzjRsfbr94y21gA23udmH5dzwLZwqi7W5CHM4

One would be remiss, not to mention how the late Rev. Jerry Falwell, founder of Thomas Roads Baptist Church and founder of Liberty University in Lynchburg, VA, left an insurance policy of $34 million dollars to the two entities he had established. Approximately $29 million of the insurance policy went to the university to pay off existing debt, with the remaining $6 million going to the church. Paying off decade-old debt, Falwell repositioned the university for an unparalleled trajectory of growth. Today, Liberty University is one of the largest and fastest growing private universities in the United States. Imagine the possibilities for your family and your church if you would leave a million dollars behind after you pass away! Even if one could not afford these things in life, perhaps one can provide for them in death, through an insurance policy.

FUNERALS

"The Israelites grieved for Moses in the plains of Moab thirty days, until the time of weeping and mourning was over" (Deuteronomy 34:8 NIV).

Unlike many wishes that can be made binding upon a family after the death of an individual through a will, funeral arrangements are not typically included or enforced by a will. One may express certain desires in a will, but because of the turnaround time between an individual's death and the time it takes to probate a will; one might have already had a funeral and been buried. However, one can have their desires recorded in an affidavit, post-mortem letter, letter of wishes, meeting minutes, or by making a recorded or public statement. Yet, understand that none of these instruments make funeral arrangements legally binding on the family. It does at least put your desires on record without everyone guessing at or debating your final wishes.

"Now Samuel died, and all Israel assembled and mourned for him; and they buried him at his home in Ramah..." (I Samuel 25:1 NIV).

Matters such as location(s) for memorial services(s), order of service, speakers, singers, song selections, eulogist, burial location or disposition of remains can be addressed in writing prior to one's death.[55] Some years ago the trend was to pre-pay for funerals and burial plots. However, with many funeral homes closing, merging, or not willing to honor previous agreements or prices; pre-paid funerals are no longer viewed as a preferred option. Yet with the cost of inflation and speed to which many quality cemeteries are filling up, it still remains a good practice to purchase burial plots in advance. Moreover, even if you cannot control the details of your memorial service, most family members will respect one's choice of a pre-paid burial plot.

"And Joseph made the Israelites swear an oath and said, "God will surely come to your aid, and then you must carry my bones up from this place" (Genesis 50:25 NIV).

"Moses took the bones of Joseph with him because Joseph had made the Israelites swear an oath. He had said, "God will surely come to your aid, and then you must carry my bones up with you from this place" (Exodus 13:19 NIV).

PRESIDENTIAL STATE FUNERALS

Few know that one of the first items on the agenda for a new president is the planning of their own funeral. Even if you were not born in the 1960's, most have seen or remember the numerous images from the funeral services of President John F. Kennedy taken only days after his assassination. Typically, presidential funerals are planned early in an administration.[56] Lessons learned from the Kennedy assassination,

---

[55] I recall how one of my great aunts had everything paid for and planned for her funeral: pictures, floral arrangements, outfit, casket, obituary, order of service, headstone, and burial location. The only thing she left empty before the funeral was the space for her date-of-death and of course, her space in the casket!

[56] Ironically, President Kennedy had not planned his funeral at the time of his death.

presidents are under the constant threat of someone taking their life.[57] Moreover, there is recognition that in order to plan all the events and ceremonies for the presidential state funeral, it cannot be crafted at the last minute. The prestige, pageantry, and precision required for a successful state funeral must be choreographed way in advance of it ever being needed.

While not equivalent in position, many cultures and denominations plan funerals for pastors, bishops, and heads of church denominations (as well as their spouses) that in many ways mirror presidential state funerals. Presidential state funerals can last 5-10 days with services held in their home state, the Nation's Capital[58], and at their place of final burial.[59] According to the White House Historical Association,

"By helping plan their own funeral, presidents are able to incorporate personal touches that can elucidate their character and legacy on a national stage for the last time. In many ways, funeral services are final conversation with the nation, and illustrate something about the man and the way in which he wishes to be remembered."

If presidents can plan ahead for their funeral, should not a pastor, pastor's spouse, diocese or jurisdictional prelates, or a presiding bishop do the same? If more did so, perhaps it could help alleviate some of the stress and anxiety off of one's surviving spouse, family, congregation, and denomination. In closing, remember and reflect upon the words from the final sermon by late Rev. Dr. Martin Luther King, Jr. given two months prior to his assassination.

---

[57] More than 30 attempts to kill an incumbent or former president, or a president-elect have been made since the early 19th century. https://en.wikipedia.org/wiki/List_of_United_States_presidential_assassination_attempts_and_plots Retrieved July 15, 2020.

[58] President Nixon's state funeral in 1994 did not include a trip to Washington, DC.

[59] Presidential state funerals can be declined by the former president or by the president's family.

"Every now and then I guess we all think realistically about that day when we will be victimized with what is life's final common denominator-- that something we call death. We all think about it and every now and then I think about my own death and I think about my own funeral. And I don't think about it in a morbid sense. And every now and then I ask myself what it is that I would want said and I leave the word to you this morning.

If any of you are around when I have to meet my day, I don't want a long funeral. And if you get somebody to deliver the eulogy tell him not to talk too long. Every now and then I wonder what I want him to say. Tell him not to mention that I have a Nobel Peace Prize--that isn't important. Tell not to mention that I have 300 or 400 other awards--that's not important. Tell him not to mention where I went to school.

I'd like somebody to mention that day that Martin Luther King Jr. tried to give his life serving others. I'd like for somebody to say that day that Martin Luther King Jr. tried to love somebody. I want you to say that day that I tried to be right and to walk with them. I want you to be able to say that day that I did try to feed the hungry. I want you to be able to say that day that I did try in my life to clothe the naked. I want you to say on that day that I did try in my life to visit those who were in prison. And I want you to say that I tried to love and serve humanity.

Yes, if you want to, say that I was a drum major. Say that I was a drum major for justice. Say that I was a drum major for peace. I was a drum major for righteousness. And all of the other shallow things will not matter. I won't have any money to leave behind. But I just want to leave a committed life behind. And that is all I want to say. If I can help somebody as I pass along, if I can cheer somebody with a well song, if I can show somebody he's traveling wrong, then my living will not be in vain."[60]

---

[60] -- Martin Luther King, Jr., "The Drum Major Instinct" Sermon delivered on February 4, 1968 at Ebenezer Baptist Church, Atlanta, GA, (At the request of his widow, these recorded words of Dr. King's last sermon were played at his funeral on April 9, 1968l) https://genius.com/Martin-luther-king-jr-his-own-eulogy-2nd-block-annotated Retrieved July 15, 2020.

CHAPTER 15
NOT LETTING PEOPLE KILL ME OR DRIVE ME CRAZY: PASTOR'S HEALTH AND WELLNESS

Although this book was written to help leaders prepare for succession, it is important that leaders take the necessary precautions needed to avoid needing a successor anytime soon. "I am preparing for death but don't plan on dying anytime soon!" The grace and anointing on your life will help a leader do seemingly supernatural things. But unless you are Elisha, there is no power in your dead bones. Nor will you be able to teach your disciples for 40 days after your resurrection, before your ascension like Jesus.

Thus, if a leader is not careful, the weight of ministry can crush a minister. Needless to say, the saints will kill you, shout at your funeral, find your replacement and forget that you ever existed leaving behind a grieving widow and family to live life without you. Leaders must do what is necessary to maintain good mental, emotional, physical, and spiritual health. One may say, well, when it's my time, it's my time. However, it's no need to check out of the hotel room before checkout time, either.

A recent study[61] found Methodist ministers to have higher cholesterol, higher rates of asthma, and more hypertension than other Americans primarily caused by obesity. The study found, "Forty-one percent of United Methodist pastors are obese, says Proeschold-Bell,

---

[61] PASTORS FACE A GROWING HEALTH CRISIS by Aaron Earls - May 24, 2018 https://factsandtrends.net/2018/05/24/many-pastors-face-a-health-crisis-a-few-simple-tips-can-help/

compared to 29 percent of all Americans." The study also noted stress, depression, and financial worries as other causes of poor health.

The authors looked at four factors that distinguish pastors who flourish from those who burn out.

(1) Focusing on the big-picture mission rather than outcomes (collection plate or church attendance).

(2) Having a lot of social support also helps. Pastors who do well have more friends and closer relationships than pastors who don't.

(3) Have good professional boundaries and still have friends. Flourishing pastors are able to have good professional boundaries and still have friends.

(4) Thriving pastors also pay close attention to their health—both physically and spiritually. They have plans for regular exercise and regular prayer and devotions.

(5) Ministry can be all-consuming. The pastors who thrive learn how to draw some clear boundaries around their time. Sometimes the best thing a pastor can do is to get some rest.

Our prayer is that you will live a long, healthy, and successful life. That God will grant you wisdom and favor as you lead and plan for the future. And when the time should arise that your mantle is passed, that it will fall into the hands of someone who will double your works, complete your vision, and lead the people to a land of promise!

PRAYERS OF ST. THOMAS AQUINAS

In closing, I leave you with two prayers by St. Thomas Aquinas, "Pour forth your brilliance upon my dense intellect, dissipate the darkness which covers me, that of sin and of ignorance. Grant me a penetrating mind to understand, a retentive memory, method and ease in learning, the lucidity to comprehend, and abundant grace in expressing myself...Grant me, O Lord my God, a mind to know you, a heart to seek you, wisdom to find you, conduct pleasing to you, faithful perseverance in waiting for you, and a hope of finally embracing you."

CONCLUSION

As you read this book and begin to think about your succession and estate plans, hopefully you will be motivated to take action. However, a leader should be warned, and even admonished, not to allow their own haste or impatience to have an heir to cause them to give birth to an Ishmael. In examining Genesis 12, God appears to Abraham (Abram at the time) and informs him "unto thy seed will I give this land" (Genesis 12:7). In Chapter 15 God reaffirms his promise, "After these things happened, the Lord spoke to Abram in a vision. God said, "Abram, don't be afraid. I will defend you. And I will give you a great reward" (Genesis 15:1 ICB).

Rather than rejoicing because God was going to build a great name and inheritance for him and his family, Abraham's response was not very enthusiastic or appreciative. "But Abram said, "Sovereign LORD what can you give me since I remain childless and the one who will inherit my estate is Eliezer of Damascus?" And Abram said, "You have given me no children; so a servant in my household will be my heir" (Genesis 15:2-3 NIV).

On one hand Abraham should be commended for his forward thinking. As any good leader, Abraham is thinking about the future. "God, I am getting old and what good is it to make me wealthy if I do not have anyone to pass it onto when I die?" While Abraham does quibble about being childless, in general, he more specifically asked God about the lack of an heir. Abraham asks God if the steward of his house, Eleazar of Damascus, would be the heir to his wealth. God responds, "This man will not be your heir, but a son who is your own flesh and blood will be your heir" (Genesis 15:4 NIV).

Many of you may know the rest of the story. The bible says that Abraham initially took God at his word, believed him, and figured that somehow God would make His word come to pass. Abraham and his wife Sarah, after an additional ten years of waiting, however, both began to believe that the clock had run out on them, or at least Sarah, to have children (Genesis 16:2 KJV). Sarah believed that God's promise could still be fulfilled by Abraham and devised a plan to offer her handmaid, Hagar, to produce an heir.

Consequently, the plan worked, so they thought. Abraham now 86 years old, finally had a son, Ishmael. (Genesis 11:27-12:6). Other than Sarah hating Hagar for getting pregnant by Abraham - mission accomplished, right? However, there was a minor detail in the fine print that God omitted from the initial covenant: God's blessing was not just on Abraham to be the father of many nations, but also for Sarah to become the mother of many nations. I could imagine the confusion that Abraham could have experienced.

"Wait? What? After I violated my vows to my wife, get another woman pregnant, and have a son that is now old enough to legally become my heir; you tell me that my wife, Sarah, is going to have a son, and he's going to be the heir?" (Genesis 17:1-22). Hence, Sarah at age 90, and Abraham, at age 100, welcome into the world their son, the promised heir, Isaac. Consequently, Sarah demands that Abraham put Hagar and Ishmael "out on the streets" because she doesn't want controversy over the rightful heir to Abraham's wealth. Abraham kicks Hagar and Ishmael out, forcing them to survive on their own, with only "a loaf of bread and a bottle of water" given to them (Genesis 21:1-21 KJV).

Why is this story of Ishmael important to leaders? First, a leader must be reminded that God does not always operate on the same schedule as ours neither is God bound by the limits of nature. Under most circumstances, Abraham at eight-six years, was probably right; he did not have much more time left and needed to birth an heir real soon. However, what Abraham did not know, which God did, is that he would live to reach his 175th birthday. Hence, Abraham thinking he was running out of time, had not even reached middle age yet! Furthermore, Sarah at age 76 years old would live to be 127 years old. By nature, most successful leaders are impatient, task-oriented, and resourceful. However, when it comes to God and his promises, we cannot rely solely on our own schedule, plans, or devices. Leaders must not get ahead, nor behind God, but learn how to move with God.

Secondly, leaders must be careful with whom they listen to and take advice from during the succession planning process. By faith, Abraham heard and heeded to the voice of God to leave his kindred for the land of Canaan (Genesis 12:1-5). Abraham knew God's promise to give his seed the land of Canaan (Genesis 12:6-7; 15:18). Yet when it came to having an heir, Abraham listened and capitulated to Sarah's carnal recommendation rather than to consult God. The same Sarah that suggested Abraham use Hagar to bear a son, immediately got jealous of Hagar when she became pregnant. Moreover, it was Sarah that forced Abraham to put Hagar and Ishmael out. Therefore, a leader cannot allow their spouse, family, or congregation to force them to make a move or decision that is not sanctioned by God. Some of the same people who rush or dictate to the leader who they should select as an heir, may end up being the most critical and divisive afterwards.

Thirdly, a leader must be careful not to force someone into the position of "heir" when God has not designated them to receive the inheritance. Abraham was impatient, made a rash decision, and took matters into his own hands without first consulting God for all the details. Ishmael had the position of heir, but Isaac had the promise. Make sure we trust God to provide an heir of promise and not an heir of promiscuity. Because of Abraham's "I must have an heir now" syndrome - he leaves behind a trail of damaged relationships and complications that we notice in the world today. This is not an indictment of Ishmael or Hagar; God, in fact, made Ishmael successful and even a great nation (Genesis 21:18). However, he was not the promised heir for this particular kingdom.

Lastly, the split between the two sons could ultimately cause generations of unnecessary strife; the consequences could be far greater than who gets the property, church, or business. Without Abraham's poor decision, Isaac would have been the sole heir to Abraham's inheritance without thought or challenge. Generations later, the children of Ishmael and the children of Isaac are still fighting over "Abraham's inheritance". Leaders, please be proactive in preparing a succession plan, but also be willing to wait on God to provide the "heir of promise".

APPENDIX 1
SUCCESSION PLANNING CHECKLIST

- o Have you identified your successor or developed a process to determine your successor?
- o Is the successor or succession plan documented in your church bylaws or some other document?
- o Does your church have a constitution, bylaws or discipline manual?
- o Do your by-laws also address the possibility of the pastor becoming temporarily or permanently disabled?
- o Do you have 2-3 names on the church bank account? Do 2-3 people have knowledge of all bills, debts, liabilities, or financial obligations held by the church?
- o Is all church property properly deeded, titled, and recorded in the name of the church? Where are these documents located? Who has access to them?
- o Have you started training and developing your successor?
- o Do you have adequate health and disability insurance?
- o Are your intentions regarding end-of-life medical treatment officially documented?
- o Has the person you want to make health care decisions for you been properly documented?
- o Do you have a Will?
- o Do you have a Power of Attorney?
- o Do you have a Living Will or Health Care Directive?
- o Have you started saving for retirement?
- o Do you have adequate life insurance? Is the premium paid and beneficiaries properly documented? Does someone have knowledge of their existence especially if there are multiple policies held by different entities for different purposes. (For example, health insurance may provide a "complementary" life insurance policy sufficient to cover funeral expenses. In addition, the pastor

may have one policy to care for the church and a different policy to care for their family) Does someone know where the policy is located and have access to it when you pass away? (If in a safe deposit box at a bank, does this person know which bank and are they listed as someone who can have access to it?)

o Have you made arrangements for your spouse to receive your salary after your death?

o Have you made your funeral arrangements? Do you know who will pay for your funeral?

o In the event of disability or death does someone have your password or other login credentials, including answers to security questions, to access e-mail and social media accounts, electronic devices, cloud-based services, and other online services or accounts? Likewise, does more than one person have this information for church accounts. proceeds, tangible property and more to the rightful owners. (Note: each year states seize millions in "unclaimed property" - money, stocks, bonds, dividends, utility deposits, insurance proceeds, tangible property, etc. because the owner forgot about it or the heir(s) did not know anything about it.)

o Have you had your annual physical or check-up with a doctor in the last 12 months?

APPENDIX 2

Key Questions for Succession Planning in Church Bylaws

1) Do you have articles of incorporation and bylaws? How often are they updated? Where are they located? Do they address the issue of succession? Do you record meeting minutes, in some format? Where are they archived? Who has access to them?

2) What are the laws in your state regarding non-profit organization or church? Does state law address any of the potential issues related to succession planning?

3) Does the denomination have a say or role in determining the successor? Are there provisions that govern succession planning in the denomination's bylaws, discipline manual, or doctrine book? Are these provisions in harmony with your church or do they conflict or contradict each other? If there is a conflict, which entity or set of rules would have supremacy?

4) Do your bylaws address the role, responsibility, and rights of certain title or position holders as it relates to succession planning. For example, assistant pastor, co-pastor, executive pastor, senior pastor, pastor emeritus? Do certain titles automatically vest into other roles upon the death of the pastor?

5) How specific are the bylaws regarding the succession? Is the successor automatic based on a previous position or title held? Will there be a selection process from a pool of qualified candidates?

6) Who manages the selection processes – ministers, deacons, trustees, or a select or special committee? If trustees, are they valid, current, and recorded with the appropriate authorities? If a

selection committee, how are they selected or is it by virtue of holding a particular position in the church? Is there a "period of mourning before the process begins? Is there an overall time frame for auditions, voting, and installation?

7) If there is an election, who gets to vote? How do you determine membership? How often do you update membership records? Age of voters? Good standing?

8) What type of vote or majority is required – unanimous, super majority, simple majority, plurality?

9) Is there a process for declaring the current pastor incompetent, temporary or permanent disabled or incapacitated?

10) What is the scope or limitations on an assistant pastor, co-pastor, interim pastor, acting pastor, pastor emeritus when a pastor becomes disabled or is deceased? How much authority do they have in the interim period between the disability/death of a pastor and the selection of a new pastor?

11) Even if a pastor can appoint someone as next the pastor, does this decision or appointment have to be approved, voted upon, affirmed, or ratified in some official manner? How does it become official - pronouncement and laying on of hands, a written and signed declaration, or official installation service?

12) In the case of a reformation or denomination, how is a successor selected? Do the other bishops (if there are any) decide? Does the person who succeeds them as pastor also succeed them as presiding bishop over the organization.? Alternatively, do the other pastors or members in the organization, fellowship, or network

have a voice or vote in the selection process. Does the denomination have terms, term limits, age limits, or post-term roles term duties for past leaders? If a leader passes away during their term, does the successor complete the term or hold it until an election can be held? Does completion of the predecessor term count towards their term or are they entitled to their own full term and term limits?

This is not a complete or exhaustive list of everything a church needs to consider in crafting its bylaws. It is important to consult an attorney that specializes in non-profit entities or churches that can help craft the appropriate language. Moreover, an attorney that can understand and be sensitive to church the history, doctrine, and polity of each church or reformation. If you desire a consultation, the Law Office of Travell Travis, PLC is available to assist you. Our contact information is included in this book for future reference.

APPENDIX 3
CANDIDATE EVALUATION

Instructions: For any response less than a 3, please provide a rationale for the score and a recommendation for how the candidate can improve in that area. Score each according to the following scale: Strongly Agree (5); Agree (4); Neither Agree nor Disagree (3); Disagree (2); Strongly disagree (1); or Not Applicable or No Basis to Evaluation (0)

1. Age: I believe that the candidate is at the right age to become pastor.

   Rationale:

   _____

   _____

   Recommendation:

   _____

2. Trustworthiness: I am very comfortable with disclosing private and confidential matters with the candidate.

   Rationale_____

   _____

   Recommendation:

   _____

3. Character: The candidate has strong character and has no known personal issues that could potentially disqualify them from becoming pastor.

   Rationale_____

   _____

   Recommendation:

   _____

4. Doctrine: The candidate shares my doctrine and biblical views.

Rationale:

_____

_____

Recommendation:

_____

5. Vision: The candidate shares my vision and priorities for the church.
   Rationale:

_____

_____

Recommendation:

_____

6. Leadership: The candidate has demonstrated strong and effective leadership skills.
   Rationale:

_____

_____

Recommendation:

_____

7. Reliable and Dependable: The candidate is both reliable and dependable.
   Rationale:

_____

_____

Recommendation:

_____

8. Calling: I strongly believe that the candidate has been called to be a pastor.
   Rationale:

_____

_____

Recommendation:

_____

_____

9. Congregation: I am confident that the congregation will be
   enthusiastic and fully support the candidate as their next pastor.
   Rationale:

_____

_____

Recommendation:

_____

_____

10. God's Choice: I am absolutely certain that the candidate is the
    person that God wants to lead the congregation, next.
    Rationale:

_____

_____

Recommendation:

_____

ABOUT THE AUTHOR

Bishop T. Travell Travis, Esq. is a native of Martinsville, Virginia. He was saved and called into the ministry at the Shiloh Way of the Cross Church, under the leadership of his father in the gospel, Bishop Earley Dillard. Bishop Travis received his B.A. from the University of Virginia with a double major in History and African American Studies and a minor in Religious Studies. He received his J.D. from Howard University School of Law.

Since 2003, Dr. Travis has been employed by the Hampton University James T. George School of Business. Dr. Travis teaches various courses in entrepreneurship and business law. From 2004-2017, Dr. Travis served as an assistant dean for the School of Business. A published scholar, Dr. Travis is a past recipient of the Hampton University Chancellor and Provost Teaching Innovation Award and the Hampton University Academic Excellence Award.

In 2005, Attorney Travis opened the Law Office of Travell Travis, P.L.C.; a general practice law firm. The firm represents pastors, entrepreneurs, creative, and the community. Attorney Travis is admitted to practice law in the Commonwealth of Virginia and the District of Columbia. He is a member of the Apostolic Law Association. He regularly presents seminars on entrepreneurship and various legal matters. His educational videos on these subjects can be found on social media.

Since 2009, Bishop Travis has served as the founding pastor of City of Refuge Way of the Cross Church in Richmond, VA. Within the Way of the Cross Church of Christ International, he serves as general counsel and is a member of the board of bishops and trustee board. From 2007-2019, Bishop Travis served as the 9th President of the International Youth for Christ. In 2018, Bishop Travis published his first book, *Don't Eat the Baby: The Characteristics of a Cannibalistic Church*.

Bishop Travis and his beautiful wife Sherina D. Travis (Mason), of Philadelphia, PA. reside together in Richmond, Virginia, with their three daughters: Deonna, Janiyah, and Amiyah.

www.travelltravis.com
Instagram and Twitter: @travelltravis
Facebook and YouYube: Law Office of Travell Travis, PLC